PRAYER WARRIOR
THE LIFE OF A SEER
THE SPIRITUAL WARFARE SERIES
LEVEL FIVE

SUDIE LANDRY

Cypress Cove Publishing

PRAISE FOR Prayer Warrior

Walking by the Holy Spirit is a genuine way of life. However, not many can be found guilty of walking out this level of life. May you allow Holy Spirit to use this collection of stories to encourage your walk to the level of life God intends for you.

Christy Boutte, Co-founder of Covenant Spotlight Magazine, Lafayette, LA

Simply Motivating! Sudie writes some fabulous books on prayer and family. They are super motivating attention-getters. What a Glorious Calling! I especially love how she pulls together the stories with Scripture!

Tiffany with KAJN-102.9 FM, Crowley, La.

I love this book because it reminds us that God is always available and always willing to speak to us when we open our hearts to Him and trust His voice. It doesn't matter how big or how small the matter. We can cast all our cares on Him because He cares for us (1 Peter 5:7). Knowing that He hears and He speaks and He moves for us all the time is so critical, especially in this time and season. We must be keenly led by His spirit, just like Sudie Landry.

Nedra Epps, www.facebook.com/Vision-Heirs-Publishing-and-Consulting

This book is filled with so many testimonies of how God speaks to us, answers our prayers, and shows up in ways that we least expect Him to. This book is very encouraging and enlightening on Gods goodness and how He speaks and operates through people just like you and me.

Jacquelin Hatley Worship; @jacquelinhatley

In her book, "Prayer Warrior: The Life of a Seer," Sudie Landry shares with her readers a glimpse into the spiritual gift entrusted to her by the Spirit of our Heavenly Father, to pray for others.

This book so beautifully illustrates that everyone needs a Seer praying for them!

Carl Comeaux
Pastor and Teacher
Drumbeat House of Bread
Lafayette, La.

What a wonderful read! This is truly a book that is easy to read and most of all, brings you into revelation of hearing from God! This is a must for everyone that is looking into the realm of seeking Him more, it is beautifully written and a must for your library.

Leigh Ballinger
Ballinger Ministries

Prayer Warrior: The Life of a Seer
The Spiritual Warfare Series – Level Five
Copyright 2020 by Sudie Landry

Published by:
Cypress Cove Publishing
PO Box 91195
Lafayette, LA 70509-1195

Paperback ISBN-13: 978-1-936707-35-5

Library of Congress Control Number: 2020906112

• Edited by Neal Bertrand
• Interior design by Jeremy Bertrand, Cypress Cove Publishing

The Spiritual Warfare Series by Sudie Landry

◊ Silent Prayer: A Spiritual Journey Toward Exposing the Occult – The Spiritual Warfare Series – Level One; 6x9 paperback, $14.95
◊ Trail of Six Roses: Supernatural Events at Mother's Funeral – The Spiritual Warfare Series – Level Two; 4x6 paperback, $6.95
◊ Mom Bradley's Crossover: From Deathbed to Heaven – The Spiritual Warfare Series – Level Three; 6x9 paperback, $8.95
◊ Supernatural Encounters of the Godly Kind – The Spiritual Warfare Series – Level Four; 6x9 paperback, $14.95
◊ Prayer Warrior: The Life of a Seer – The Spiritual Warfare Series – Level Five; 6x9 paperback, $14.95

Other Titles Published by Cypress Cove Publishing

Down-Home Cajun Cooking Favorites; 6x9 paperback, $14.95
Rice Cooker Meals: Fast Home Cooking for Busy People; 6x9 paperback, $14.95
Slow Cooker Meals: Easy Home Cooking for Busy People; 6x9 paperback, $14.95
Cajun Country Fun Coloring and Activity Book; 8x10 paperback, $4.95
Fun Times Puzzle and Activity Book; Mazes, Word Search, and More; 8.5x11 paperback; $9.95
Fun Times with Math-Logic Puzzles: Sudoku, Kakuro, & Gokigen; 6x9 paperback; $9.95
Fun Times Cajun Puzzle & Activity book; 108 activities; 8.5x11 paperback; $9.95
A House for Eliza: The Real Story of the Cajuns; 6x9 paperback, $15.95
Never Say Goodbye: Real Stories of the Cajuns; 6x9 paperback, $14.95
From Cradle to Grave: Journey of the Louisiana Orphan Train Riders; 8x11 hardcover, $26.95
Dad's War Photos: Adventures in the South Pacific; 6x9 paperback, $19.95. Also in hardcover from Amazon.com for $29.95; and in multimedia Kindle ebook format.
Louisiana Legacy: History of the Daigle and Schexnayder Families; by Edward Daigle; 6x9 paperback, $19.95
Grow Up Into Him: Bible Word Studies to Live in Victory; 8.5x11 paperback, $19.95
The Real You, My Beloved: Seeing Yourself Through God's Eyes; by Michel Lanclos; 6x9 paperback; $9.95

**Visit CypressCovePublishing.com for all of our latest books.
To order, see our website,
or call Toll Free (888) 606-3257,
or buy from Amazon.com.**

Contents:

Prayer Warrior contains a large number of real life stories of miraculous answers to prayer, the intervention and workings of the Holy Spirit to bring defeat to the enemy and victory to God's people.

PAWPAW'S VISIT

It was a sad time for me. My grandfather had just passed away in Arkansas from cancer. The phone call of the dreaded news came, and I would not be able to attend his funeral.

My sister and I had gone to visit with him by bus a few weeks earlier. His children were there also and each in our own way said our last goodbyes. At least that is what I had thought.

Now I was on the phone being informed of the funeral arrangements. After I hung up the phone, I went and laid down on my bed. Memories of this wonderful person in my life brought a smile to my face as the tears began to fall from my eyes uncontrollably.

My grandfather was over 6 feet tall and very thin in stature. My grandmother who was tiny and short measured barely 4 feet 6 inches tall. It was a sight to see them together anywhere that they would go.

Their marriage had gone through seasons of together, and seasons of being separated from each other. After only a few years together, they divorced.

I asked my grandmother why she had divorced my grandfather, and she said, "I was young and immature. He did not buy me the yellow house that I wanted, so I thought that he did not love me enough." So, she packed up her belongings along with their young son and infant daughter to start a new life without him.

They stayed apart for six years. During this time my grandmother met a nice man, and together they had a son.

My grandfather remarried also, and he and his new wife had six children. Ironically, they both lived in the same small town and would see each other at the store or at the gas station. Both marriages soon had their problems and ended in divorce.

They found themselves wanting to be together again and decided to remarry. They bought a nice piece of property in Northwest Arkansas and soon built a new house.

PawPaw brought the three youngest of his six children to live with them. Along with her son from her second marriage and my dad and his sister, there were now a total of six young children to bring up. My grandfather supplied all their needs by working at a local lumber yard. I loved my visits with them as a child and continued visiting them into my adulthood for many years.

Now here I was, crying because I could not go to his funeral. My husband said that we could not afford for me to miss work. I was distraught. There I was sobbing and praying and thinking of the many memories of my grandfather.

Suddenly the room became brighter. As I turned my head toward the open door to see what may have caused this, I could sense a very tall presence that was now stooping to be able to enter. It then appeared to be walking toward the chair positioned across from my bed. I could see the movement, but no actual form or shape.

I asked, "PawPaw, is that you? Have you come to say goodbye to me since I could not go and tell you goodbye?"

There was no verbal reply, but a peace that surpassed all understanding made me believe that it was. The scripture reads "And the peace of God, which passes all understanding, shall keep your hearts and minds through Christ Jesus." Philippians 4:7

That night in a dream, my grandfather's smiling face with those light blue eyes bent down and gave me a kiss goodnight for the last time. The next day, I could only smile, and I still do when I think of him.

TABITHA

It was during the Christmas season of 1977 that this story took place. I had given birth to my third child, my youngest son, on Christmas Day, December 25 at 12:03 a.m. just after midnight.

He was now only two weeks old. Prior to my taking a break from my business to have this baby, I had heard the crying of a baby while I was working in my shop. There was no baby in my house or beauty shop.

By now you are aware that I do operate in certain gifts of the Holy Spirit, so you know this is when I focus more intently. I did not know who this was or why I was hearing it cry. I did know that it was coming from the spiritual realm.

I was sitting at my kitchen snack bar on the stool when the news on the television station announced that there was a statewide emergency blood drive for a car accident in Shreveport, Louisiana causing the death of an unborn baby and leaving the mother in critical condition.

The type of blood needed was rare and the blood banks were low. They gave the name of the patient. I remember saying, "I am glad that was not my sister." I was wrong, it was her. She was not using the name that I knew her by.

Moments later I received a phone call from another sister that was there at the hospital with her. We were told to come right away and to be prepared that our injured sister may not make it.

Her baby had died on impact during the accident when my sister's stomach had hit the steering wheel. She had been taking another sister to the emergency room and had run a stop sign. Her baby was due to be born the next week. The mother had named her baby Tabitha.

My youngest sister had massive internal injuries. Her doctor gave us the gloomy news that if she survived, she would never be able to have more children because they had to do a total hysterectomy, and if she lived, she would also be coming home with a colostomy bag.

I did not go see the dead baby, but my dad did. He said that she was a beautiful baby girl with red hair and looked like she was just sleeping. There was a small funeral while my sister remained in the hospital.

My sister had a long recovery time ahead for her. Two other sisters lived nearby and would have the responsibility of taking care of her. They would continue to keep us updated. I headed home to my newborn son and family.

Against all odds of her recovering, through prayer she did. After many surgeries, she did have the colostomy reversed back to normal after two years.

Things happen, and we sometimes will never understand, but I do know that something good did come out of this bad thing. She went on to take care of other people's children in different seasons of her life. She herself remains childlike in so many ways and continues to have a special playful attitude. After all, she will always be my baby sister. She was and still is the youngest of our original six siblings.

THE BARNYARD ACCIDENT

My two boys loved going to our farm where there was a real red barn filled with hay and lots of cows grazing nearby. The hayloft was one of their favorite places to play with their cousins who lived next door to the barnyard. It was on one of these weekends that I had allowed my boys to go spend the weekend with my sister-in-law and her family.

I was reading a magazine back home on a Saturday morning when I got this overwhelming sense like someone was falling from a very high distance. I felt like the air had been knocked out of me and it was hard to breathe.

I began to pray for the safety of whoever it was that may have had an accident or needed prayer. The thought that it could have been one of my boys in trouble had never occurred to me. When the boys returned home late Sunday afternoon, I did find out that it was my youngest son who had fallen out of the top hayloft door, backwards to the ground below.

I had not received a phone call regarding this incident because it appeared that there were not any broken bones or even bruises of concern. My youngest son was always accident prone because he was always playing daredevil games and he was afraid that I would make him come home. He begged and pleaded for them not to call and promised to tell me when he got home.

His story to me was that they were playing and wrestling when he fell against the loft door that they thought was latched. As he was falling, he could hear his cousins screaming for help.

My son said that he felt like he was floating and then he found himself face down with his chest hurting, and having trouble breathing. He said he felt like something or someone had picked him up from the ground and he was alright. This gave them all a big scare, so the barnyard play was ended for the day.

Prayer is always a good thing to do if you have thoughts that something is wrong, or someone needs prayer. A prayer could make a difference in the outcome.

CROSSROADS ANGEL

I shared my angelic visit in the story titled 'Heavenly Visitor' that was recorded in my book *Supernatural Encounters of The Godly Kind-Level 4*. My friend had a visit from him also the same day, but in a totally different way.

A man clothed in ragged and dirty clothes approached her as she and her two daughters were leaving the morning church service. He told her that he was hungry and asked her if she could help him. To get rid of him, she quickly pointed him toward our church food bank to get some supplies. She later found out what had been given to him as he was ushered out of the church with a small bag in hand. Sadness and regret for not helping him filled her heart.

She said that she began to feel very guilty for not taking more time to try and help him. She soon found herself searching around trying to locate him inside and outside of the church. He was nowhere in sight. She began to wonder if she had just flunked a test from God to do the right thing.

She and her children decided to pick up some lunch through a drive through location before heading home. That is when she saw him again, but this time he was standing on the highway median holding a sign, HUNGRY. There was no way that this was the same man who had approached her in church, but it sure did look like him. It was impossible for him to get where he was because of the distance, unless someone gave him a ride, she thought.

As she headed through a drive through food place, she ordered extra for him. No matter what, she would go back and give this person some food.

As she neared him and stopped her car to hand him the food through her open car window, the man said. "Thank you, Cathleen." That was her birth name that she had never used. Cathy is what everyone called her. How did this person know her real name? It did get her attention, and she knew then that this was not your everyday homeless person.

As she drove away, she looked into her car rear view mirror to find that he was no longer standing there. She knew then, that she had met an angel. Later, she and I shared our stories of that day.

BOOK COVER VISION

In 1986 the Lord placed on my heart to write my testimony of my childhood journey from living in a foster home to become part of an extended family to eventually seeing my mother who had not raised me.

The book cover idea came to me in a dream. All I saw was a white flower. The only kind of flowers that I was aware of included lilies, pink carnations, magnolias and roses. My knowledge in general was very limited. So, I decided to research the story of each flower to know if the picture would tell the main focus of my story to be written.

I pulled out my World Book Encyclopedia collection and looked under each flower species listed to learn the meaning of each flower name. I eventually found 'Lilly of the Valley'. This flower could survive the worst of climate conditions, and even grow under a rock or survive with or without sunshine or water. You could not kill it no matter how hard one could try, and yet it was beautiful. It was a survivor. This flower looks like many little white bells connected on the flower stem. This was the perfect description of the story that I would and did write later.

BLUE BUS MINISTRY VISION

I was asleep and suddenly I saw a blue bus, a Blue Bird like the school bus. In my dream I saw it parked near a building. I knew that God would reveal the meaning of this dream eventually. I went on about my daily business of running my in-home beauty shop.

I attended an Assembly of God Church not too far from my home. I loved going to church every Wednesday night and Sundays and occasionally I would attend the Saturday night service. I loved sitting in the balcony. The Pastor said that most people sat there to prevent from becoming too involved in the church activities. He was right. I knew that if I sat in the bottom sanctuary, I might join too many things.

At one of these services, a strong thought came into my head. "You need to make an appointment to speak with the Pastor." I thought to myself, the Pastor will think I am crazy since I have been hiding in the balcony a couple of years trying not to get involved. He will not even know me. "And by the way, God, what am I supposed to say anyway?"

"Ask him what the biggest need is in the church, and then volunteer to take on the project." Wow, I thought for sure I'll be thrown out of this church after this visit.

I prayed, I called, and a few days later, I did make that appointment. This was back in the 1980s. I shared with the Pastor everything above, and he just smiled and said that there was a great need to start a bus ministry. He then told me to go outside and look at the Blue Bird. I had no idea what a Blue Bird was, but I did find a white van. I went back in, and he laughingly told me to look for a blue bus.

I found the bus, and yes it did have Blue Bird written on it. Surely this was not the one he was talking about. I did not have a chauffeur's license to be able to drive this. I wasn't even sure if I could pass the test to acquire the needed credentials. Yes, he said that is the one. Well I thought, if God is with me, then everything needed would fall into place and it did very quickly.

I got the needed handbook to prepare me for the test. I studied, I prayed, and I was prepared. I went to our local Department of Motor Vehicles. Everything was going great until it was time to take my license picture. That is right, the camera broke.

According to the lady, the repairman would not be in until the following week. That would be too late for me. I needed to be certified to drive for a church field trip that same week.

Suddenly to all our amazement, in walked the repairman who said that he just happened to be in town and came to check on this location. He repaired the camera. It was God's perfect timing. It all worked out.

As I was going to pay the fees for the final transaction, the computer began to make strange hissing noises as the lady tried to key in the amount to be charged. She was baffled and seemed to be afraid to touch the keys at all. There seemed to be a lot of hissing electrical sound coming from it.

I just smiled and firmly placed my hands on that computer and prayed out loud commanding that it would begin to function properly. Lots of people witnessed as the computer began printing out the paperwork to clear me. The smile on my face just got bigger.

The cashier said that they had never experienced this kind of thing before. I told her, "When you serve the Lord, these things happen often, at least they do to me."

I now had a Commercial Driver's License and was now officially a bus driver. When God calls someone to an assignment, he will anoint and equip that person for the task. Get ready, and expect the unexpected, but know that everything will work out according to His plan for you.

I practiced driving the bus in our church parking lot. I then took it for a test drive on the route that I would soon take weekly on Wednesday nights. After making the planned location stops of where the bus would pick up the passengers, I activated the pickup route about two weeks later.

Lots of things tried to stop the bus from running, but God always sent in help or made a way to get everyone to church on time. I started the route at 4 p.m. and had everyone to church for 6:45 for the 7 p.m. service. The church service ended most of the time around 9 p.m. I returned the bus usually around 10 p.m. to park it after the night route was completed. I then routinely locked the gate to the cage that it was parked in.

At the beginning, I was picking up mostly children, but soon their parents or siblings started coming. I oversaw this ministry for one year. After that, the season changed, and other people began to get involved.

The ministry expanded to larger outreaches. I was glad that God had allowed me to be a small part in His much bigger plan for our church. There was always another season or assignment waiting for me to pursue, with joy.

HOLY GHOST HOTLINE

Over the years I had met many wonderful people whom the Lord had placed into their hearts to meet the needs of the homeless people in our area. On one of my trips to drop off items collected by me to the location then known as 'The Well,' I was informed that they had no room to take in donations at this time.

They then referred me to a man known as 'Reverend Richard.' He had a small little shack near this location donated to him and he would take on any items that The Well could not use. I drove to meet him, and this is where a new contact was created for me to take my donations to those who were in need.

Reverend Richard was once a homeless person himself and knew how these supplies were always welcomed and appreciated. He had to depend on other people to get around town since he did not own a vehicle.

When God calls one to an assignment, the needs will be met. He did not have a car, he did not have a cell phone, but he did have favor with the Lord. The needs for his ministry were always met to supply the street people.

On this day, instead of me taking the load of supplies to Reverend Richard, he told me that a friend had a truck and they would come to my house instead of me bringing it to them.

We set a designated day and time of arrival to my house which was today. They were now about an hour late and I began to be concerned that they may have gotten lost. They had no cell phone, so I could not call them. I began to pray.

My house phone rang, I answered and said, "Hello." I could hear the Reverend Richard talking. The connection had a little static, so I said "Hello" again. He kept talking and I soon realized that he could not hear me at all.

I then focused in on the conversation to discover that he and his driver were lost and trying to find my house. I listened as the driving directions were being repeated to the driver. They finally drove up after about ten minutes of me being on the phone.

I went outside to greet them. I opened my garage to let them load up the supplies that I had gathered for them. They began to share with me their problems finding my house.

I then told them that I had heard their conversation on the phone and I was giggling. Their facial expressions suddenly changed. I told them that I had heard them talking because they must have not turned off their cell phone. Reverend Richard then informed me that they did not have a cell phone and that they did not call me. Well, someone did connect us, so I guess it was a call from Heaven. This did not surprise me, but they were a little baffled.

The driver, The Rev and I prayed right then and there, and the driver repented and became a believer that day. Their ministry together lasted for many years and so did our divine connection and friendship.

WHERE'S THE LIGHT?

I was a faithful listener to KAJN, a family-owned Christian radio station located in Crowley in Southwest Louisiana. This radio ministry strengthened the beginning of my early faith journey in the 1990s. I tuned in often to listen to the teachings and to the "music with a message."

I soon found myself visiting the local Family Christian Store to purchase the gospel music that they played on air. Before long, I was purchasing lots of music and started wearing scripture T-shirts. I was a Christian, out loud and on purpose, and I was not ashamed of the gospel of Jesus Christ. A friend soon joined me, and we became well known to the store and the radio station. Together we formed 'Praise Music Production'.

As the years passed, together we promoted the local Christian music artists for free. We would organize concerts to feature these unrecorded music singers and musicians. Later, down the path, KAJN started playing some of these talents. My relationship with them and the staff continued to gain favor.

Over the years I was invited to do interviews on their talk program, 'Kajun Talk.' I would frequently call in to share a praise report of good news for myself or others. There were times to ask for needed prayer request agreement from their 'Upper Room' prayer ministry not only for me but for others. As people would ask me for prayer, I would give them the station number for them to call if they needed.

I decided to apply for a part-time job at the Christian book store. I was hired and worked the late afternoon shift three days or more a week. There I met more awesome talents as they would sing, as they listened to music demos. The store eventually decided to let me have an indoor concert in our store several months later.

We were located inside of a huge mall called the Acadiana Mall, so this was a first time for them to agree to do something like this. I was now in complete charge of this event. The one rule that had to be followed was to keep the volume down so that it did not bother the other stores nearby.

The date was decided, and the fliers were made announcing the upcoming event. We placed them in different locations two weeks prior to the actual event. Some of the other stores in the mall agreed to put the flier up in their store regarding our upcoming event.

I thought everything was in place and ready for this event, then the Holy Spirit prompted me to do a prayer walk through the mall and pray that the anointing would be so strong that it would lead people to our store.

I started the walk outside in the parking lot at the main entrance of this mall praying and walking as I had been instructed to do. As I finally reached the door to our store, the Holy Spirit then instructed me to go to our huge window display and just stand there and look in before I would enter.

As I stood there, I found myself praying that people would not just walk past the store but would stand there unable to move until they had at least heard the message in the music that would be playing.

It was time for the concert and as the music played, people of all faiths could be seen praying, some lifting hands, and others singing as they purchased items from our store.

The store was buzzing with lots of people and the atmosphere seemed different, tingly. The manager of the store then gave us the clearance to announce that people could worship in their own way as they were accustomed to. That is when the place seemed to explode with a joyful singing and verbal prayers could now be heard. Some were even kneeling and praying.

I was at one of the checkout registers when again, the Holy Spirit instructed me to look at the display window. Yes, there they were, lots of people just standing there as the music played. At the end of the song, they would leave, and another group would come and repeat the same thing. Amen! God sure does have unique plans!

We were nearing the closing hour, when a satanic occult and drugged couple approached my register and asked, "Where is the light?" It caught me by surprise, and the male asked again, "Where is the light? We have been following it since we got here."

I then remembered the prayer that I had said and smiled. I then told him that he had been following the light of Christ and that was why he was in our store. Like two puppets being operated by invisible wires, they then turned and awkwardly stumbled out of our store and then could be seen outside at the display window looking in until the song finished playing.

Jesus saith unto him, I am the way, the truth, and the life; no man cometh unto the Father, but by me. John 14:6 (KJV)

In him was life; and the life was the light of men. And the light shineth in darkness; and the darkness comprehended it not.
John 1:4-5

THE BANQUET TABLE

The Lord had opened a door for Praise Music Productions to do its first Gospel concert showcasing local singers and artists. Lots of preparation had gone into the planning for this special event. A friend and I had a heart to help those unrecorded artists get exposure for free. We did not charge for people to be represented by us. If you wanted to sing for the Lord, then you were welcome to get on our concert list dates. It was just that simple. Since it was God's idea, that list always stayed full.

Tonight was the night! The bands were already there at the Northwood United Methodist Church setting up sound equipment together for everyone to share. The event would start at 6 p.m. and go until 10 p.m. this Saturday night. My friend had agreed to go monitor and greet the people until I could get there.

My long day at my beauty shop was now ending and it was time for my second wind to kick in. After the last customer was finished, I sat down in my styling chair, I asked God for needed strength to get to the concert refreshed. I knew He would because He had helped me in that way in the past. I closed my eyes to pray.

After I had finished my short prayer, I opened my eyes and then noticed that my finger nails were blue. At first glance I thought that perhaps I had not lathered them enough, therefore leaving some of the color rinse still on that had been applied to my last customer. I then looked into my shop styling mirror and saw that my lips were blue also. "OK God, if I go by what I am seeing, then I should be dead." I was experiencing fatigue, and a headache by now, but that was the norm for me dealing with my extremely high blood pressure history. I again prayed for those symptoms to go away.

No matter what, I needed to get ready and it would only take five minutes to get to the concert which was about to start. I was greeted by my music partner as I entered the door to the sanctuary. She asked me if I was alright, and I told her to pray for me because I felt light headed and strange. She took her camera and had someone snap a picture of her and me. Later when the pictures were processed, my face was totally blue.

We were blessed with local talent and those that drove in from Texas, Arkansas and Oklahoma to be part of the first 'Just for Jesus' concert. It was a misty rainy day, but that did not stop the crowds from coming in. In between the showers of rain, cars and even motorcycles would make their way into our parking lot. Rain would come, stop and then the sun would come out.

It was now time to start the concert, so I headed for the front row to sit down. Now I could rest and enjoy how the Lord had used me and my friend to organize and showcase those singing for Him. I closed my eyes and felt a warmness cover me from my head to the tip of my toes.

My eyes were still closed as I listened to our first scheduled singer. It was then that the Holy Spirit instructed me to open my eyes and to look up on the white wall that was behind the singer. I did, and this is what I saw.

At the far-left corner near the ceiling I could see a large radiating gold silhouette of Christ in a flowing garment. I then was instructed to close my eyes. I also prayed that the Lord would let my friend see all of this and she did. I was told to open my eyes and now the silhouette could be seen walking toward the door behind the performing singer. Once the form got to the door, He stood on the side as if He was inviting me in. I smiled at Him as I looked past the singer and asked, "Lord, why am I seeing this?"

Once again instructions were to close my eyes and open them when told to do so. As I did this, I looked up to my far right of the white ceiling to see the most beautiful stained-glass window with radiating rays shining from it down onto an elegant banquet table prepared with all the beautiful place settings for a five-course meal. I asked, "Why are there no people sitting at this table?" The reply was, "All are invited to join me at this table, but only a few choose to follow."

The concert was a huge success, and I was blessed beyond my expectations. My friend and I had lots to talk about after the night was over. As for that picture that was developed, well my face was totally blue. When shown to other people, they would say things like "Bad film developing." I had a reminder and proof that God was with me that day when the powers of darkness were trying to stop me from receiving blessings from the heavenly realm.

THE OPERA HOUSE

I belong to a local writer's group in Lafayette, Louisiana. Sometimes special events are held in a nearby small town. The vice president of our organization was also a traveling journalist who had visited this location and thought that it would put a special touch on the upcoming yearly event.

She had made all of the necessary arrangements to confirm that we would be using the Opera House of Crowley, Louisiana. It had recently been restored to its original beauty and had been declared as one of the landmarks of that small town.

The front entrance looked very old and in need of repair. As my friend and I entered the doorway, we were met by a rather old dusty room with just a few brochures lying on a glass top cabinet. I gathered what I could to have reading material for later.

It was not what we had expected. It looked like a huge storage room. Odds and ends of various product displays could be seen. We were then directed toward a staircase, like in the movie *Gone With The Wind*. There was no elevator and we were told that the Opera House was on the second floor.

Once we reached the top of the stairs, and had entered through the massive door, it was as if we had stepped back into time. The view was breath taking. There were rows and rows of newly upholstered opera seats on each side. We walked down the sloping aisle toward the front of the raised stage. A spotlight was shining down on a small round table with a chair seated on each side. Our host would use that set to interview the selected guest authors for this event. It was a spectacular presentation.

Each member found their way to the section and seat of their choice to enjoy and take notes on our presentation. I chose to sit on the left side about four rows from the front. I could glance around and see who all were there.

I was intently listening to the guest author speak when I slowly turned my head to the right to spot an oddly dressed couple sitting on the opposite side of the aisle from me. The lady had on a heavy jeweled floor length dress covered with a long velvet drape held by a beautiful gold clasp. She also wore an adorned fancy feathered and jeweled hat. She was a large woman.

Next to her was a man. He was much smaller in stature and wore a French beret with his vested suit. They appeared to be of great wealth with their gold accessories. They sat very erect in posture and kept their eyes focused straight ahead. I thought perhaps they would perform for us as a special surprise since they seemed to be dressed appropriately for this room.

I would say that they were sitting for around ten minutes when they suddenly seemed to be exiting from their seats toward the aisle to leave. I looked to see if anyone else was seeing what I was watching. No one appeared to notice them at all. I turned back quickly to see the couple in the aisle, but they seemed to be floating just above the floor while moving and not walking. As they neared the top of the door entrance to leave, they seemed to just disappear. Alright, I would have lots of questions to ask at the end of the workshop program.

When the event was over, I began to ask everyone present if they had seen the couple. I described the couple and indicated where they were sitting. I even asked the people on the first floor if any of them had seen a couple who met this description. The answer to all these questions was no. Of course, I would not stop asking and did continue searching for an answer several days later.

I called the Opera House to talk and share what I had seen. The person in charge at that time told me that they had heard that there were some reports of ghostly activities, but no one had ever reported anything like this. She did say that the clothing that I described did sound like the opera costumes that were possibly housed in the museum with some other historical clothing worn in those days.

I did find out that the man seemed to fit the description of the original owner of the Opera House. As for the lady, she may have been one of the actresses that the owner had spent lots of time with.

I do not know why I was the only one who saw this, but I do know that I was not surprised.

PUBLISHER'S OPINION ON THIS "GHOSTLY ACTIVITY"

Jesus Christ said Satan is the father of lies and a deceiver. Satan wants you to believe lies and to be deceived. Such as believing in reincarnation, that we had past lives, that mediums and fortune-tellers are telling you the truth, that ghosts are dead people who often have trouble "crossing over" to the other side where they can be at rest.

NO! These are Satan's lies. According to Jesus Christ the Almighty God, once you're dead, and your spirit and soul vacate your body, God takes your spirit and soul and brings them into heaven; or casts them into hell for all eternity, where there is no escape.

Satan wants you to believe there is no penalty for rejecting Jesus Christ, therefore no eternal damnation in the lake of fire.

The two ghosts in this story, the man and woman who floated to the exit doors, were NOT the opera house owner and his consort. They were demon spirits on assignment. They were in disguise, to fool whoever could see into the spirit realm.

TOUCH NOT

This morning I woke up by an electrical shock to my right hand. This was the first of this kind of morning wakeup call for me. It was exactly 7 a.m. and time to get up to get dressed for church.

It was during our praise and worship time that I suddenly noticed sparkling and glittery particles floating in the room. It was like I was seeing those sparklers that we light up for the holiday celebrations. I was sure that I was seeing this in the spiritual realm. This means that I was probably the only one seeing this at the time.

As I looked around the church sanctuary, it was like everything seemed to be color enhanced. Each detail was much clearer than usual. Today the terminology of "High Definition" would be the perfect description. I said a silent prayer and asked God, "What is going on, why am I seeing this?" My attention was then focused on a certain lady who now was in the front praying for those who had come up for prayer. She looked familiar and then I remembered her, and then I knew why.

In one of my previous stories she had tried to place her hands on a dear friend of mine that was in line for prayer but was not able to do so. It was like an invisible wall was there stopping her each time that she tried to touch my friend. At that time, I asked, "Lord, why are you not allowing this lady to lay her hands on my friend who was receiving prayer for herself?" His reply was, "Touch not my anointed." I then knew that this lady needed prayer for unknown issues herself in her life.

Well on this morning, that lady went up for prayer for herself. As the elder began to pray for her, she dropped to her knees and started jerking uncontrollably. Our pastor did not touch her but stood behind the elder as he continued to pray for this same lady that was in my story, Heavenly Visitor, in book four, *Supernatural Encounters of The Godly Kind* where the angel had not allowed her to touch my friend who was in deep worship at the altar. He made the sign 'STOP.' It was as if an invisible wall had gone up to prevent the lady from touching my friend. Her faith walk had been questionable to many of us.

There definitely had been a Divine Intervention that day. The Lord had spoke to my heart that when the timing was right, this lady would be delivered from all false doctrine and that her 'playing Christian' days were now over. She would have a new and true faith walk.

My friend and I were led by the Holy Spirit to also pray for this lady that sat near us. As we prayed, I started experiencing the taste of blood in my mouth. The taste seemed to get stronger as we continued to pray. We had smelled this odor before, but this was different. I started to stop our intercession, but the Lord instructed us to continue.

On our way home, my friend and I discussed this experience. She said that she could now smell the blood scent was now on me and she now has the taste of blood in her mouth. We did not get a clear revelation of why this was happening to us, or what was wrong with the lady. We knew that we would have to study more on the issue of blood in the Bible and wait until the Word of God would give us clear understanding.

We eventually found out that she had a serious female illness and a blood disease. The taste of blood in our mouth and scent of blood was the Holy Spirit giving us what the Bible calls a "Word of Knowledge." It is one of the Gifts of the Holy Spirit in 1 Corinthians chapter

12. She did receive prayer later in her church for healing.

ROOTS AND THE SHOVEL

Not all stories I recorded are long. This is one that started as a short instant picture as I laid down to sleep.

I volunteered at a local Christian radio station at this time. The DJ was a nice man. For the purpose of this story I'll call him "R". He had an awesome country sound to his voice. He was a full-time employee. He would later go on to become a minister.

I saw R with a shovel in his hand digging and digging and digging in this dream. I asked the Lord, "What is he looking for?" The Lord replied, "He is trying to get to the roots." I did not understand at the time the meaning of this dream. I do now. We all have things in our lives that we need to address, clean up or remove completely. Little did R know then that God was leading him down the path to become a Pastor.

Let me just say, first came the Christian radio station, then a Christian woman, then marriage and then ministry. It was his destiny and in God's plan and timing.

SONNY BOY

I had just closed my eyes to sleep when another of those short visions appeared. There was my Aunt Lela and my recently deceased and buried grandmother sitting together. Aunt Lela looked so happy and Little

Mother so nice in the dress that we had bought for her. She had her legs crossed and had a beautiful smile.

I then noticed the stained-glass windows behind them with rays of light shining through on them. I then saw my brother, Sonny, walking back and forth past this door. He would try to enter, but the door seemed to be locked. He made several attempts. They were on the inside looking out. He was on the outside trying to get in.

I asked my grandmother, "What is he trying to do?" She replied, "He is trying to find a way in." Two weeks later, my brother died. He had gone home with a headache and several days later, his body was found. They said that it looked like he just went to sleep. His body was cremated and scattered by his children in Arkansas, the state that he loved so much.

THE ACCIDENT

I was blessed to have met a Jesus truck-driving lady named Judy M. She was my mentor in my early walk for the Lord. She was a natural redhead, as I am. Anywhere she would go, she could be seen reading her Bible. She was a witness to all who met her.

She had two daughters and one son. The son was almost angelic in appearance. He had that kind spirit and he was good looking also. His mother and my children would go on swimming outings together. He was wonderful to kids and young adults.

I suddenly felt like something had hit me in my chest and I sprang up as I was awakened from my sleep. His mother's name, Judy M, came to my mind. I found myself praying for her or whoever it was. I then tried to go back to sleep. Here was another one of those short visions. I would soon find out the meaning.

I received a phone call to let me know that he had been coming back from a late job and fell asleep and hit a tree and crushed his chest. He died on impact. This news sent my friend into a deep depression, but she continued to witness for the Lord.

She later experienced breast cancer, survived, and then she had a stroke and is now in a wheelchair. Even though they say she does not always know who is speaking to her, I always ask, "Judy, do you know who I am?" She always replies, "Of course I do, Sudie." She is now in a nursing home, but still smiling even though she cannot talk at times.

UPDATE: Her loving daughter was her caregiver up until her death in 2019. She will always be remembered by her sweet smile and her love of the Lord. She always had her Bible with her ready to share the Word of God.

GRANT'S VISITOR

Grant, my two-year-old grandson was playing in his room when his mother went to check on him. I'll call her K. My daughter-in-law at the time asked him who he was talking to. He then told her that Maw-Maw Kelly was not sick in bed anymore. He said that she was there playing with him. My mother-in-law, his great-grandmother had passed away a few weeks earlier.

Grant had only seen her one time and had gone to the hospital with his dad and mother just before she had died. Naturally this really shook up Grant's mother who was not accustomed to hearing stories like this.

K then decided to tell my son Toby the incident but went on to say that he talked about dead relatives from her side of the family that he had never met. My son then shared some of the stories that he and I were part of together.

My grandson never told me this, but K did share with me and so did my son Toby. Things like this started happening with my son Toby at an early age also. As for me, I guess all this fruit does not fall too far from my generational tree. I have been experiencing these kinds of things since I was five years old.

DEEP POCKETS

Once again, I close my eyes and up pops this television screen. I see my close friend Frances digging in her pockets. She keeps trying to pull something out. Her pockets seemed to be empty.

I ask, "Lord, what is she trying to do?" He replied, "She is trying to find more money."

My friend was always the go-to person if her children needed anything. She always tried to do without, but never said no if they sounded like they were in need. Now that she had become a new widow, it seemed like they were more in need than normal.

Money seemed to be spent like pouring water out of a glass. I was concerned but tried to keep my mouth shut. It got to a point that I questioned her if she was keeping track of all the money that she had and was spending since her husband had passed away. This was only into maybe six months of her widowhood. She had no idea. She had not even been balancing her books monthly like she used to.

When this vision came to me, I knew then that I had to tell her. She did get the meaning and even today when she is spending or lending too much, God gives her the reminder of this vision to guide her in making good decisions.

THE LUNCH GUEST

After church one Sunday, I decided to go for lunch afterwards to a local nearby Ryan's Restaurant. After serving myself some nice portions of their wonderful food, I then sat down to enjoy my selections.

I tend to be a people watcher and soon focused my attention on a Pentecostal family that was being seated by the restaurant host. You could tell by their clothing style that they were of this faith. The family unit seemed to be all there. The father, mother, teenage daughter, a boy around 10 years old, and a baby still nursing a bottle, gender unknown.

There was another teenage girl with them also. She was of dark hair and complexion who seemed very uncomfortable, as if she did not want to be there at all. She must have been a guest, for the family were of light hair and complexion. I could sense that there was also something very odd about this young lady. She seemed to have a darkness around her.

The baby soon began to cry, and the mother tried coaxing the brunette girl to hold the baby. The girl pulled away and then finally held her arms out to hold the child. Then I saw it began to happen. A manifestation of an evil spirit was beginning to show up on the young girl. My skin suddenly was covered with goose bumps. Something evil was about to happen.

I kept my eyes focused on the girl, and soon began seeing her features change. I was now seeing an evil skeleton face peering down with red glowing eyes at this innocent baby that she now held while the rest of the family moved away from the table toward the serving line. I began to pray for protection for the baby so that the girl could not touch or hurt it. Her hands suddenly had long nails that looked like curved claws of a hawk ready to pounce on its prey. Just as she was about to touch the baby's face, the mother returned, and the girl's features returned to her natural lifeless facial expression.

I prayed and watched this family until they were finished with their meal and were up and leaving. I sensed in my spirit that this young girl had suffered severe abuse from the occult side. She needed serious prayer covering. I continued to pray that the love of this family unit would help her overcome whatever unkindness that she may have been subjected to in her young life.

As they were exiting the restaurant, the girl turned, and it was then that I saw a beautiful smile on that once downcast face. She seemed to have a glowing light radiating from her face. I believe that she went home with a new-found peace and joy added to her existence. Only God could have made this possible.

I never saw that family again, but I choose to believe that the girl did get the love and help that she needed. I know that God had a reason for me to see and pray and be there on that day for that reason. Prayer is never wasted.

EVIL SPIRIT OF INCUBUS

My 102-1/2-year-old great-grandmother had just passed away and we were all gathering at my grandmother's house to attend the funeral. All five of her daughters were there, and J.R. her only son had not yet arrived. We made coffee and got dressed while waiting for him.

All the daughters were in their 90s. J.R. was the eldest of the six making him around 96 years old. He finally drove up and it was then that I got to meet him. Just by his first hug, I found myself cringing and pulling away. "Oh Lord" I found myself thinking; he is not who he appears to be. His presence made me very uncomfortable. He seemed to want to touch and get too close to me when he thought others were not looking. Not good! I found myself avoiding him every chance that I could.

I was taking a needed coffee break at the kitchen table. He was always showing up. He seemed to be following me everywhere. He asked if I believed what was written in the Bible. I found that to be a rather odd question since he had professed that he was a Godly man of faith. I gave him my answer, "Of course," and then got up to go stir the large pot of soup that I was cooking. This was just an excuse to get away from him and any further conversation that he was trying to continue.

To my shock, he had followed me to the stove and when I turned, we were face to face. Too close! He was now pushing me against the cabinet trying to plant a kiss on my lips. I turned my head quickly and he got my cheek. What? What was he doing? I pushed him away and he said, "Just one kiss on the lips will not hurt anyone." I again pushed him away and made sure that I would not be caught again in that situation with him in any room. Should I tell my grandmother about what her brother was trying to do? I chose to tell her nothing for now.

Great-grandmother was laid to rest and the family members began returning to their homes out of state, including J.R. which sent a huge sigh of relief throughout my whole being. I stayed a week longer, to visit and restock her cabinets before leaving for my home state of Louisiana. I had not yet mentioned anything to my grandmother about the advances from her brother but would when the right time came up.

It was two nights before I was going to leave that I had a frightening visit from an invisible evil spirit that literally got into bed and laid down next to me.

It was bedtime and I was exhausted and ready to call it a night. I was saying my prayers as I usually do nightly. I was laying on my left side. Suddenly, I heard a loud grunting sickening sound in my right ear. The mattress seemed to have a sinking sensation of something slithering and sliding into my bed and settling next to me, too close. Hot air could be felt as the grunting was getting louder in my ear. "Oh My God," I cried silently, "this is a satanic manifestation in bed with me!" The name J.R. came into my thoughts. I struggled to verbally sound the words out audibly to command the spirit of lust to flee. After several attempts to scream it out loud, I finally was able to and the demonic presence left immediately.

The next morning around 9 a.m. the telephone rang. I answered the phone. It was J.R. I told him that his sister was nearby, and I was going to hand her the phone. He said, "No, it is you who I want to talk to." He continued to tell me how he felt about me and how he saw himself in bed with me last night, sharing the details I wrote above word for word. I stopped him and told him that I was handing the phone to his sister. They had their conversation.

A few minutes went by and J.R. called again. As he started to talk, I informed him that if he continued bothering me, that I would tell his sister what he was doing to me. I hung up and he then called again. My grandmother had not been in the room but did hear the phone ringing and had asked who was calling so much. She saw the look on my face and asked me what was wrong. I told her.

She then shared with me the details about her troubled brother. Even though he was married, in his youth he was never faithful to his wife. She also said that he talks like a Christian but lives the life of evil and was known to have gotten into witchcraft activities. I was so glad that she was not upset with me and was sharing these details.

I told her everything about the bedroom visit and then we both bowed our heads and prayed for him. He did call back again, but this time she answered the phone. I left the room for her to have a long conversation with him privately. He never called me again.

That was my first and hopefully my last experience of what one would call an incubus. This is an evil thing and should not be pursued to have the experience. Only God can protect you if you should find yourself face to face with this evil force. Get into the Word of God and get grounded. It is your only protection. You will need it.

NOTE FROM THE PUBLISHER:

As Sudie stated above, J.R. had gotten involved in witchcraft. This disturbing event described here is extremely demonic and involves leaving his body as in astral projection, along with spirits of sexual lust and incubus.

RADIO PROMOTIONAL

In the 1990s a friend and I had the idea and passion to promote unknown talented Gospel singers and unsigned bands. We did everything that we could to help these anointed ministers of music. We did it free at no charge and with joyful hearts. Concerts were already being done by us.

She and I visited weekly at the nearest Christian store to listen for new talent and to look for scripture T-Shirts and music for our listening pleasure. As people came to purchase their music, they would sing, and bingo, we heard awesome talent. It was very easy to get people on our list. We showcased them free and they performed free. It was a win-win situation.

We could not afford to pay for any radio or newspaper promotions at the time but would eventually. We did the best with what we had with the Favor from God on our side. Our list of talent continued to grow. Different locations opened up for us to let them perform. Our name then was Praise Music Production, a name given to us by God.

I listened to my favorite Christian Radio Station, KAJN. On this day as I was listening to this station, I got excited when I heard a promotion regarding a local talent announcing an event that was coming soon. I wanted to know more so that I could get connected to help spread the word too, so I called the station.

I was told that the promotion was ready but had not been aired yet. How could that be? I had just heard it on their radio station, and shared details of what I had heard. They said yes, that I had all the information correct, but that the station had not aired it yet.

This is the way that KAJN became familiar with my name when I called, and I did call a lot. Little did I know that they would be hearing more from me soon. To this day, KAJN Radio Station in Crowley, Louisiana is my favorite Christian station to listen to.

The Lord did open a way for us through this station to promote our local Christian songs and authors. My grandmother always told me that if you have God and a good name, then that is all you need, and your needs will be met. I needed to be able to promote our talent on the radio. I did not have the money to meet the costs charged for air time to make this happen; at least not yet.

I made a phone call and was transferred to speak to Barry Thompson, the owner of this station. I quoted the above phrase, and he said, "In that case, I guess we need to help you." They did help me then and continue to this day to be a huge blessing in my life as God takes me down the different spiritual paths.

OUIJA BOARD

My kids were now at the age of getting past the stage of playing the usual children's board games. They wanted to try new ones out on the market, such as Dungeons and Dragons and, of course, to experience the Ouija board, (pronounced weejee here in the South).

The church that we were attending believed that these were games of the occult. They taught us that participating in games like this could pull us into the areas of the satanic occult activities. People today still deny that the demonic realm exists and that all Christian people are just crazy, or brain washed. I am here to share that it does exist and is very evil.

In my early Christian walk in the 1970s, I really did not understand the seriousness in playing these kinds of games. Later as I was personally exposed to witchcraft attacks, I met people who used to belong to these satanic groups. I would learn the truth.

I later would come to learn that my church had given me and others the true warning to stay away from things in this area. Lots of those adventures are now recorded in my 'Spiritual Warfare Series' now published and available on Amazon.com. Just type in "Sudie Landry" in the search box on Amazon, and my books will come up. They are all supernatural encounters against the demonic realm. By faith and God's Word is the only reason I survived to write all these stories.

I learned to stay away from tarot card readers, psychics, and mediums because they were not of God. I soon found myself on the path of researching to discover what local stores had these games for sale, especially the Ouija board. I soon located a Toys R Us that had the Ouija board on their shelves, along with the Dungeons and Dragons game. I made a trip to check them out for myself. I prayed for protection before going; this is always a must-do.

I can still clearly remember the details of that store visit. It was at night right after closing my beauty shop around 6 p.m.. This store was then located inside of our local mall. I went straight to the front desk clerk who was working that night and asked where the games were located.

This young man looked to be around 17 years of age and this was probably his first job. He was very polite and gave me directions to the aisle where the games would be. Since he appeared to be the only employee working this shift, he quickly returned to his front counter to greet potential customers.

I soon also noticed that I was the only customer in the store. This place was usually packed with parents and children browsing. Something was off, and I began to get this uneasy feeling. This happens when I am about to have a supernatural encounter of the evil kind.

Goose bumps were now covering my whole being. Yes, the Ouija Board was near. Like a warrior getting ready for battle, I inhaled a deep breath, said a prayer, I then braced myself for what was coming. It did, but in a way that I had never experienced before. As I took my first step toward the aisle, I looked, but could not see the board games that I was looking for.

I turned back to go get the clerk to show me where they were, when suddenly, boxes of games came flying off the shelves on their own, hitting the floor loudly. It made such a clanking noise that the young clerk came to see if I was alright. He thought that I must have fallen.

As he looked at all the games on the floor, I explained that I did not do that, and that they had come flying off by themselves. Of course, this sounded crazy to him, but I knew that it was the truth and I was sticking to it.

He put the games, and all the Ouija boards back on the shelves. Before he could walk away, once more they came flying off the shelves again. I could see how he was now really shaken and very scared, but he managed to put them back into the designated spot. He then returned to the front desk once more, as I stood there to pray against all sales of this dangerous game.

As I neared the front, the young man asked me if I could stay with him until the next shift came in and admitted that he had never experienced this kind of stuff before and did not want to be alone. I did stay and shared with him why I believed that the games should not be sold in any store. The games flying off the shelves convinced him of that.

As soon as the next shift person came in, the young man told him of our experience. I never saw that young man or the Ouija game in that store. That was many years ago, and I assure you that I did check often.

THE FACE OF CHRIST

It was now the day to go film some music performances for a friend at his bar for future promotions. My cameraman had been a good friend of this entertainer for several years. He and I were producers at our local Community Media Television Station. We had the privilege of using the television cameras outside of the studio if we turned in some video footage of the project. This was never a problem for us since we were always filming something going on in our community. This was my first filming inside of a bar, but this bar was not open for business.

This establishment once belonged to the young entertainer's father, who had passed away several years prior to this taping. It was run down, but the one room still had the original bar counter and mirrors still standing with a few memorabilia from the past still seen hanging on the frail walls.

As the cameraman was setting up the camera equipment and sound system, I looked for a place to set up my one camera that I would use to capture the whole stage performance. I found a stool behind the bar counter. I would use it to stand on to film when it was time. It was then that I began to have a personal conversation with God. Why had I agreed to accept this assignment? Then in my spirit I heard, "You are here for a reason."

As I was looking down from the stool that I was now standing on, I suddenly saw the huge glowing silhouette of the face of Christ radiating from the floor. Now wait a minute! Am I really seeing this? This did not seem right. I turned my face away and then glanced back and that is when the young man was standing in the spot where the face once was. I knew then that this was a message to be shared with him when the time was right.

This entertainer was well known as a radical and was involved in many projects to save the planet. I would learn more about him in the future.

We finished up our filming and now were packing up the equipment and putting it all back into their cases, when I turned to see a huge outline of an Indian on the tattered wall just behind the stage that the performers used. I knew that I was now seeing into the spiritual realm. I asked myself, "Why am I seeing this, and should I tell Drew?"

As we were getting ready to say our goodbyes and leave the building to head home, that huge glowing face of Christ showed up again and so did the Indian figure.

Alright, I need to tell Drew now and see what comes out of this. I turned to Drew and shared with him what I was seeing. I told him that I did not know what it meant but was to tell him what I was seeing. He answered, "I know what it means."

He shared that his sister had just passed away, and he had been praying about something. He said that my message gave him his answer. To this day, I do not know, and do not need to know what the message was. It was a personal message from God to Drew.

I have been in many strange and odd places, but God always has His reason for my being on these assignments for His purpose. I just say "Yes, Lord" and follow his lead when prompted. It is always amazing to witness what he does while I am there.

The Lord is allowing me to be a servant delivering the message to those who are in need to hear from him. That is His business, not mine. His leadings always become an awesome inspirational story to share with others. For His Glory only, I write.

THE TOUCH

I operated a beauty shop in my home for over thirty years. It allowed me the freedom to talk to my customers on different subjects of interest, including my faith.

Many people of different faiths came to my beauty shop. I chose to wear Bible scripture T-shirts as my daily uniform. Each shirt worn was of a different quote from the Bible, usually the King James version. If a person wanted to talk faith, my shirt let them know that I was open for conversation or even a prayer if they needed.

I learned to wait and not force open a conversation of religion unless the customer was receptive to the idea. It was the perfect time to use the gift of healing on this lady of faith of another doctrine.

This lady was of the Roman Catholic faith. She had been a weekly customer of mine for years and years. Her children were coached softball by me and her husband was my General Practitioner until his death.

I was aware that she had been suffering with a very painful rash that could be seen on her legs and arms for several weeks. In the past, she had never asked for prayer from me, but had shared how she had prayed her rosary for me and others. Prayer is always appreciated.

It was on this special morning that the Holy Spirit prepared me, telling me that she was going to ask me to pray for healing from the rash. I had gotten her rollers in and she was now placed under the warm dryer.

As I turned to walk away, she asked me to pray for her. As I bowed my head, and kneeled to pray, the Holy Spirit instructed to touch only two places on her leg. I placed my hand just below the knee and again just above the ankle. From the knee cap to the ankles was covered in that horrible rash.

I knew then that the Lord was going to clear up those two spots and the other rash would stay. I could not tell her this, she would have to see it for herself. In

His perfect timing, the rest of the horrible raw looking rash would be gone also.

The following week she came for her styling appointment. Even though I was anxious to ask if anything happened after I had prayed, I knew that I had to wait for her to tell me. Before I could finish setting her hair to place her under the hairdryer, she said that she had something to tell me. My heart jumped with joy for I knew it was going to be a God thing.

She continued to say that she had noticed that where I had touched her leg in only two spots that the terrible rash and pain was now gone. She asked me how that could be even possible.

I then shared with her that it was the gift of healing and the Lord wanted her to know that He did it and not me. She said, "Alright, then could He please do the same for the rest of the rash and for all rash and pain to leave also?" I told her that any healing was because of her faith that had made her well.

We both bowed our heads and I prayed out loud. The following week, there were no more signs of the rash and all the pain had left her body completely. It never did return. God always comes to meet those in a way that they will know beyond the shadow of any doubt that He is real and that He is still in the healing business.

THE MESSAGE

It was during the 1980s that I decided to join the Children's Ministry at my church. I had been attending this church for a year. During that year, I was led by the Lord to organize and run the first bus ministry. I was picking up and taking home children mainly from low income neighborhoods on Wednesday nights.

Being around children came natural to me. I had plenty of patience and a noisy bus did not stress me out. I did however like to have fun with the kids, but also had rules that they learned to follow. For example, we sang, talked, laughed, and then there was the quiet zone. There was a small bridge that was just around the corner before reaching our church destination. I would stop the bus just before it, wait until there was total silence, and only then proceed. It always worked. The kids had respect for me and I had the same for them.

Now here I am sitting in the large room listening to the Children's Pastor, and soon found that I was having trouble focusing and listening to what he was preaching. I began looking around and soon noticed that most of the children were not paying attention. "If I am bored, then what are the children getting out of this?"

This question stayed on my mind. That night, the Lord decided to give me some ideas by showing me a slide show of thoughts. He showed me the faces of three clowns. Then he had them singing, playing, pulling each other and mingling with the children. Now of course, the word of God was spoken. "Lord, I asked, what are you wanting me to do now?" Then the slide show would repeat itself until I would open my eyes. After three nights of this, I said, "Ok Lord, then you send the people to me who are to be part of this assignment."

I soon shared with a close friend what the Lord had placed in my spirit to create. He then shared with others. By the next Sunday, I had a six-foot-tall lady with a stout build, and a tiny lady midget approach me and ask if they could be part of God's plan for the Children's Ministry. Well, that was a definite confirmation from God.

We set a meeting date to discuss the plan and when it was to take place. They informed me that they already had clown costumes. We needed names, and I told them that God had supplied them also. The tall clown would be Jangles, the midget would be Jingles, and I would be Joy.

Joy would speak God's Word while the other two clowns would play with the kids. We then decided that the following Sunday would be the day to crash the Children's Church morning service. We prayed together and then headed home.

Meanwhile it is bed time again, and the Lord was not finished with His plan for us on this given Sunday. "Ok, Lord, I have not attended this church for long, and after we do this surprise visit, I will probably be thrown out of church for good."

With these thoughts on my mind, I heard the Holy Spirit speak to my heart, "Ask the Children's Pastor when the service is over if he got the message." Oh wonderful, I can't run, leave or hide after, now God wants me to ask this question to a Pastor! I said, "Yes Lord."

If I wanted any sleep, I knew to just submit and go along with His guidance. I then asked the Lord to please tell me what I was going to say based on scripture and the short play that obviously was going to take place on this Sunday.

He then reminded me that this room was a cafeteria for special events. It was then placed into my heart to center it around that story to the kids as "The Bread of Life."

Ministry time! All three of us clowns came to the morning service dressed in full costume. We entered through the back trying not to be seen before the surprise entrance. We decided to go hide and pray in the women's bathroom.

We got there early to pray and share what the Lord had planned for us to carry out. We were to wait until we would hear music coming out of the room, and then we were to rush through the door with laughter, smiles and giggling. We did just that!

Jangles had a blanket that Jingles was now being dragged on and doing silly clown things. The children were laughing and clapping, everyone except the Youth Pastor. He appeared to be in shock. He stood there strumming on his guitar quietly while waiting to see how to participate in this surprise presentation.

The main Children's Pastor was not there yet. Now it was time to tell the children a story from the Word of God. I began with how this room served as a real cafeteria for special events. However, today, they were going to get a special kind of food, God's Word, which would give them the Bread of Life.

I can't tell you the exact words spoken by me that day, but I do remember clearly that as I began to speak the Word, the Youth Pastor also began to play background music on his guitar and the other musicians followed.

Then it was time to leave. I announced to the children that if they would like for us to visit them again, to be sure to tell the Children's Pastor. I thought

I was free of facing the Pastor and giving him the personal message myself. I was wrong.

Whew, we were back into the hiding place. Now to get undressed and go to the adult service; but no, God had a different plan, of course. Not enough time. We had to go now or miss the sermon. We did go to listen to the message.

We sat in the balcony, the darkest section of the church, hoping not to distract the preacher while he was sharing the message and scripture for today. We soon found ourselves praising and worshiping and not concerned of how we were dressed. After all, the Lord does say in His Word to come as we are. Well here we are! After opening my eyes, I then saw that my Lead Pastor was smiling up at us from his podium below.

Church service was now over and time to exit out the church and building as fast as we could, if possible! That was my plan, but no! Here I come face to face with the Lead Children's Pastor. He approached me and then immediately passed me. "Whew, guess I do not have to tell him the message," I was thinking and hoping. I was wrong again.

The Holy Spirit said to go get him and ask him the question. I turned and walked rapidly to catch up with him. I took a deep breath and then tapped him on the shoulder. He turned around. I then said, "The Lord told me to ask you if you got the message?" He replied "Yes," and walked away with a smile.

I then turned around to come face to face with my Church Pastor, and confessed to him who we were, and he then replied with a smile, "I am not surprised."

That was the only time that we pulled this kind of stunt, but we did become part of the first puppet ministry to be started there soon after. The Children's Ministry continues to grow and lots of laughter, field trips, fun events, and plays continue, and God's Word is taught.

I take no credit but am truly honored that the Lord used me in a small part of getting His Message to the right person that day.

SET APART

There were many trips to Arkansas with my friends coming with me. That yearly trip to visit my grandmother always brought new stories back to share with others. Our trips consisted of adventure, heavenly visitation and revelations, and sometimes even demonic attacks. It would depend on which friend or friends came along.

One friend would bring laughter and fun times. The other friend seemed to always pull out the demonic ungodly experiences. I was starting to think that our three-person trip would soon become individual trips.

There seemed to be an increasing jealousy forming within one friend, and I soon realized that it had to change. I was seeking the Lord on this. The following story came alive with meaning only within the last ten years. Sometimes revelations do not come right away.

It was a beautiful day. A day that seemed perfect for traveling and enjoying the beauty of this Arkansas landscape. Here we were playing our Christian music, laughing, sightseeing, when suddenly, the sky lit up with an illuminating unusual brightness.

We watched as there were bright rays coming down from the sky, one at a time. There was one, then, altogether there were two, then three, then there were four rays to be seen.

I pulled the car over to park, for there was something divine about this picture in the sky. We could feel that this was from heaven. Now there were five rays! It then turned into a huge hand. We all saw this and began to rejoice with excitement!

It was the Hand of God in perfect form especially for our viewing pleasure. We were all laughing like little children. Wow, what a blessing to be in His presence!

It was now time to head back to grandma's house. The sun was starting to go down. It had this crimson color and seemed to be vibrating as it was coming down slowly. There was the whole sun, then it divided into two, then it divided into three.

We were all seeing this in the spiritual realm. The Holy Spirit spoke to my heart, "There were three, then there were two and now there will be one. I have come to set you apart." I had no idea until many years later what the revelation would be to the full meaning of this vision. We all saw it, and I shared with the other two friends what the Holy Spirit had spoken to me above.

As years passed, my two friends gradually took separate paths away from our close trips with the Lord together. My stories and adventures continue. There is a season for everything as recorded in the Holy Bible in Ecclesiastes chapter three. I miss those times, but I am enjoying the new season that I am in now. Memories can always make you smile or cry. I choose to smile.

NIGHT VISITOR

My husband had just returned from an oilfield land assignment as the sandblasting supervisor after working for seven straight days. He was extremely exhausted and had just fallen to sleep to get maybe three hours of sleep when the phone rang. His work was calling for him to report back to work and requested that he was to leave immediately.

He was now tired and mad and lacking needed rest. This also concerned me that he could possibly fall asleep on this lonely drive back to the same land job location. He had no choice but go on this job since there was no other person qualified to supervise.

It was now around 9 p.m. and I was getting ready to retire for the night. I took my bath, and I am now lying in bed saying my prayers. After they were completed, I turned over to lie on my stomach. It was then that I thought that I had heard the front foyer door open. I was assuming that it was my husband returning from the cancelled job. I was wrong.

My bedroom door rarely was closed. On this night, however, it was wide open. I voiced verbally, "Merlin, was your job cancelled?" without turning over to see him. There was no response.

I then felt the sensation that a body had flopped down on the end of the bed. Then I heard the dropping of heavy shoes, one at a time. Still no response. Then a spirit of fear came upon me. This was not my husband returning, and whatever it was, it was not human.

I began to pray for it to leave. The weight on the end of the bed lifted off and then I heard walking back toward the foyer door and then the sound of it closing. This was not my husband.

A few days later, my husband returned. I asked him if he had come back to the house at all, and he replied "No." He would not understand even if I shared this experience with him. He was not interested in stories like this, so it would be a waste of time to share the details of the encounter.

Now, I do want to add that I have had many experiences of this nature before, and this was an evil spirit of some kind. I had prayed, and its unwelcomed presence had left my room. I did not get any further revelation as to why this happened, other than it did take place.

ROOTS OF UNFORGIVENESS

Here was another night of my husband and I going to bed angry with each other. No conversation and no intimacy. Our marriage vows of over forty years was falling apart. I no longer knew if I could endure this union, this "until death do we part" idea. My heart full of love that I once had for him was now being torn piece by piece from my being. I just seemed to not be able to overlook some of his cruel actions toward me and our children anymore by keeping quiet.

No matter what I tried, I seem to always get only the ugly and negative words coming daily from a very unhappy person. I had learned to just call out silently in prayer to God for constant help and divine intervention. My children chose to either hide in their rooms or go outside with their friends until their dad was in a better mood.

I had no idea just how bad it had become to deal with his mood swings or what to say or not to say. I did not like the resentment coming from him since I was supposed to be a Christian and love him unconditionally. My walk of faith was strong and his was not.

Our home was divided, and not in a good way. I continued to do my best to just go on with life and hope and pray that eventually things would get better.

My life as a child was always led by my faith that things will get better if I prayed. Now I was in a marriage that I knew had been a mistake by the time that the honeymoon had taken place. "Oh well, I made my bed and I will lie in it." I just wasn't prepared to have so many trials.

Within the first two years of marriage, I realized that my husband had not married me for love, for I was his rebound from a failed relationship. I was truly in love with the idea that someone really loved me and wanted to take care of me. I was wrong.

I paid for the rings, the gas to get us to his mom's and a job to help buy groceries. I now realize that I was an enabler. I had started our life out with this one big mistake. However, all those ashes of misery made my faith walk even stronger, and I sincerely learned what it was like to truly "Wait upon the Lord for help" by praying and waiting for the help to come.

I thought I was hiding my woes from our children but was very saddened to learn that they had seen through my falling tears that I was not alright, and that the tears were not because I was just tired, the excuse that I always used.

I was always searching the Bible for verses that would answer any questions that would help me understand my present turmoil. I had heard many sermons on 'We need to forgive in order to be forgiven.' This was the one area that I needed help in; to forgive this mean man for his constant verbal abuse.

Now back to this night and the rest of the story. As I lay there on my side of the bed on my back and hands folded in prayer, I began to pray for help to forgive this man. He was now sound asleep within the first five minutes that his head would land on his pillow.

I was laying on my back with my feet at the end of the bed, and my head near the headboard. Suddenly, something had entered the bedroom and I found that my feet were being bound, like a rope being tied to them. The wrapping continued up to my waist and arms. I am literally bound and can only move my head. I looked over to my left to see that my husband seemed to be unaware of this movement.

I was not scared, but I did silently ask God, 'What is this?" His answer was, "Roots of unforgiveness." I then heard in my spirit, "This will paralyze you from doing what I have called you to do."

Then the BIG QUESTION. "Do you want to live like this with resentment tearing you down for the rest of your life?" I said "NO!" I truly meant it, and at that moment, the vines of restraint began to loosen and untie me. From that moment, I truly had forgiven my husband.

My life continued with lots of trials, but God always met me where I was when I would reach out in prayer for his DIVINE INTERVENTION.

ANGELIC SINGING

This night I closed the door to my bedroom that connects to the foyer hall in my house. When walking out of my bedroom as you would turn immediately to the right, you would find yourself entering directly into my kitchen and den combination. This night I had gone to bed with so much troubling my mind. I was so tired from the day's work schedule, but still wanted to attempt to pray for certain people and needs during my prayer time before sleep.

I had my bedroom door closed because my youngest son would come in and out at all hours of the night. With our bedroom door open, any person coming in from outside would be able to see straight ahead into our bedroom.

Since birth, my youngest son would sleep all day and stay up busy and noisy all night while the rest of us would attempt to sleep.

I was exhausted and needed a good night of sleep to work in my beauty shop that was connected directly to my house the next morning. I have been the sole provider of my family's needs since my husband self-proclaimed himself to be disabled, which the government did not agree. Either way, the bills were all mine to take care of.

This night I was almost too tired to pray and requested something that I had never done. I prayed, "Lord please put angels inside my house to minister and take care of us." He did above and beyond my expectation.

In the wee hours of the morning, I was awakened by singing that seemed to come from my kitchen and den area. I heard voices singing and beautiful music, that I had never heard before. It sounded happy and cheerful with many voices laughing and singing. I thought perhaps it was my Christian radio station that I had neglected to turn off. I was wrong.

The Holy Spirit spoke to me and said, "Remember that you had asked in prayer for angels to come into your house to minister and protect you and your family?"

It was an angelic choir. They were singing songs of praise. I woke up the next morning with a smile on my face and well rested. Amen!

THE CARPENTER

My friend Priscilla loved to ride and enjoy the scenic view while on our June vacation. If we had plenty of money to put gas in our car, any destination was good. It was on one of these afternoon adventures that we found ourselves in a totally new unfamiliar area. We had gotten so caught up in admiring the beautiful landscape of mountains and winding roads, that we soon found ourselves near the Oklahoma border.

Each year we would visit my grandmother, usually the first week of June. Sometimes we would bring our children, but this was not one of those times. Priscilla was seeking a word from God and needed spiritual rest. Arkansas was the place that we would go to be refreshed and rest and listen to my grandmother's soothing stories of the past. After this morning visit, we decided to go riding and explore the mountain sights. We always took time for a good visit and breakfast chat with my grandmother to start the day. While we were gone, she would rest or crochet on a blanket that she had started.

While driving for a few miles and enjoying the beautiful mountain views, my friend and I soon spotted a sign off the highway that suddenly caught our attention. We pulled off into the small gravel entrance that was secured with a padlock. We could see small cabins lined up side by side a few feet apart on the uphill winding path. We saw two unfinished log cabins. Each had a sign in front announcing coming attractions. One would offer a fruit and vegetable stand, and canned products. Priscilla and I wanted to get a closer look even though it was not open to the public.

It was a cool brisk day as we stood admiring the village scenery. We were very glad that we had heavy jackets on. Even though the sun was shining bright, it was always colder in the mountains.

Just as we were about to cross under the locked metal gate, a gentleman seemed to appear out of thin air with long hair, overalls and a radiant smile to greet us. He had crystal piercing blue eyes and a beautiful smile. We told him who we were and admired the property and hoped that this village would be open to the public soon. He informed us that it would be free to the public to enjoy when finished. One learns to always take a light jacket when in the mountains of Arkansas, even in June. Just in case it would be needed. But he did not have one on.

This man with those bright blue eyes looked and acknowledged me, but then directed his attention toward Priscilla. His eyes seemed to be looking directly into her soul. It was as if he could see all her pain that she was carrying from a very abusive marriage. He then reached out and took her hand and said, "I am supposed to be a farmer, but I am a builder." As he did this, I knew then that this man was perhaps an angel with a message from God speaking to us.

A peace and warmth seemed to embrace both of us. He looked at me and nodded a "yes" to the scripture I was thinking: "Be not forgetful to entertain strangers: for thereby some have entertained angels unawares." Hebrews 13:2

He then took my hand and warmly closed his around mine, briefly looking into my eyes. He then turned back to Priscilla, looked into her eyes, nodded an understanding look, turned to walk back up the trail from which he had come from.

Priscilla and I were at a loss for words for a few minutes afterward as we reflected on what just happened. We felt the presence of the Holy Spirit. We shared our thoughts with each other regarding this encounter. He had no coat in the brisk mountain air, yet he had very warm hands and rolled up sleeves. His bright blue eyes and radiating smile brought a peace that seemed to radiate about him. We were warmly welcomed even though we were unannounced strangers on his land.

And he spoke the prophetic word, "With Faith You _Can_ Build a Bridge" over my friend who had come to rest and get direction from God. We had both received comfort by this visit. God did reveal the meaning to her later.

Questions entered our minds as we discussed what we had just experienced together. What if we had looked at his hands, would we have seen the nail-scarred hands of Christ, or was he just a messenger on an assignment from the Heavens?

A year later another friend traveled with me and wanted to go see this place where Priscilla and I had seen the man and the village that was supposed to exist. Yes, she and I did find the same place with the padlocked metal gate, but there was no sign of any log cabins. It looked desolate.

I did question people in the nearest town but was informed that there had never been any plans or cabins and that the land was owned by Quakers known not to mingle much outside of their village.

God came to meet my friend and I in a way that we know beyond any shadow of a doubt, that we had experienced a divine encounter and it must have been for our eyes only. We went looking again the next year, but still no cabins.

SPIRIT IN THE CHIMNEY

This happened many years ago to my prayer partner friend. She had lots of knowledge dealing with white and black magic in her past before becoming a Christian. She had learned many of the potions as she would visit the supply stores for these practices. She said that since she was now a Christian, she would work against the spells by praying protection for the people that needed it.

I, on the other hand, had no knowledge at all regarding any witchcraft or occult practices. I soon found myself thrust right into its midst, and she seemed to have all the answers. This began a new season for me, learning what was and was not of God. She soon began to go on vacations with me and my friend Priscilla. This is when I began to learn my lesson on how doors can be opened to be used against you; not doors of God, but the demonic realm.

I remember telling God, "With one friend I have angelic adventures with lots of laughter and rest. With the other friend, demonic encounters seem to come out from the pits of hell against me."

There was always a story to tell that would develop from each trip. The laughter I welcomed; the demonic, I dreaded. I would get a life lesson from it, and hence more stories to be shared. I soon learned that the three of us could not vacation together. So, I began to plan trips with them individually.

The chimney story takes place in the home of the friend who seemed so in tune with past occult experiences. She had told me that this spirit was a man, and that he was harmless. At this time, she was married and said that her husband did not really know or want to know anything about this.

She seemed to find it funny, but I did not. Every time that I would walk past this fireplace, I would get goose bumps, especially when I was there alone. She had never voiced any fear and seemed to welcome the unknown presence. A few months after her husband passed away, she soon began to have men come visit her. That is when things began to change and the fireplace noises at night started to concern her.

Being who she was, she waited until she felt threatened by the spirit before she called me for prayer protection. She could not tell me what was happening but asked me to have the Lord show me how and what to pray against. After a moment of me silently asking God to reveal to me how to pray, I suddenly knew. The spirit in the fireplace was mad at her. "Why Lord?" It was not happy with the men coming in and out of her house.

I shared with her what the Lord had placed in my spirit and began to pray against the spirit. The Holy Spirit directed me to pray for the spirit to leave and to be set free and return to where it had come from. She said that she could feel the presence when it left the room. The room temperature changed from cold to warm. She never mentioned him again as the man in the chimney.

TRANSFERRING OF HEALING

The day was now turning into night. One of my sisters and I had made a 3-1/2-hour drive to spend the weekend with our two younger sisters in North Louisiana. We would usually go visit on a Saturday morning and then depart on the following Sunday early afternoon.

It was not often that we could all manage to get together. The day usually passed fast with visiting other people or just sitting and talking. Sometimes we would make a trip to the nearest grocery store for something to add to a meal. The day always passed unbelievably fast.

It was now Saturday night and we had all settled down on the floor, sofa and or a chair in the living room to relax before getting ready for bed. Soon everyone was having their drinks of wine or beer. As the drinks went down, topics began to come up. As a professing Christian, I was not comfortable when this happened. I always wore my scripture T-shirts, so occasionally I would be targeted for my faith.

It was cool weather, so I had kept my light jacket on to try and prevent this from happening even though we were inside. Sure enough, someone said, "Okay, you can take off that jacket. I know that you have one of those Jesus shirts on." I did. As I took off the jacket, the room temperature seemed to drop suddenly. I felt an unwelcome presence enter in.

It was then that everyone turned their interest to me. I felt like I had become a huge target, and everyone was taking turns trying to provoke me. I felt like I was at one of those Hollywood parties being roasted. I managed to laugh and pray silently, and at the same time asking God how to respond or not to respond. It was then that my youngest sister asked me to pray for her.

I thought, 'Great, Lord, what about those that do not believe as I do? Do I pray out loud or silently?' Of course, the Holy Spirit said, "OUT LOUD." So, I stood up and went to the sister who had asked for prayer. I noticed the looks on the other sister's faces. Were they questioning or mocking? I was not sure.

As I stood in front of my sister holding her hands, she shared that she had lumps in her breasts and they hurt very bad and she wanted prayer for healing. As I began to pray, I was instructed by the Holy Spirit to tell her to take her own hands and place them on the areas where the lumps were. She did. Then I was instructed to tell her that I was transferring the anointing of healing from my hands to hers to be healed. And that when she was healed that it was not because I had prayed, it was because she had believed.

After this was spoken and done, I looked around the room to see others with tears falling down their cheeks. Nothing else needed to be said. The Holy Spirit had now cleared the coldness out of the room. The drinking was over. Goodnight hugs were given, and we all exited to our designated sleeping quarters.

The next morning over breakfast, my youngest sister had a smile on her face and her eyes seem to twinkle as she shared loudly for everyone to hear. "Sis, I got up this morning and for the first time in months, I do not hurt, and the lumps are all gone!".

I smiled and replied, "And what do you say?"

She then repeated, "It was not because you prayed, sis, but because I believed that I no longer hurt and have been healed."

Amen! No lumps or pain ever again from that day on. She was healed.

HOSPITAL ANGEL

I soon lost count of how many times I have had to make trips to the emergency room due to a severe blood pressure attack. It had become routine for me to work all day in my beauty shop from 8 a.m. to 5 p.m. and later make a trip to the emergency room to be put on an IV to bring down the blood pressure.

This was done at least two times a month. They always called me Mrs. IV and would usually let the newbie take my vitals only to watch them squirm and run for another blood pressure kit to double check the pressure reading. Eventually, I would try to warn the intern prior to the taking of the pressure so that they would not panic.

On any other given night, I would normally drive myself, but this night my head was pounding so hard, and I was dizzy and having trouble walking. I asked my husband to drive me. He tends to drive extra slow during a crisis, and I needed to get there fast. After a slow drive to get there, we finally reached the Charity Hospital, a local hospital where people go that have no insurance. He dropped me off at the emergency entrance and then drove off to find a parking spot.

As I struggled to walk to the admit desk, I kneeled on the floor and became very nauseated. Someone came behind me and helped me into a wheelchair. I was briskly rolled into the admit area where my blood pressure was taken immediately. The reading was now 232/132...Stroke range.

I began to throw up white foam. As I was heaving, I was praying for God to go ahead and take me, for this pain was almost unbearable. My husband soon found me and came and sat down beside me. I was now in the waiting room area with other patients. The wheel chair had now been taken from me to help someone else.

I laid my head on his lap to use it like a pillow. My name was eventually called to go to a room. As I got up to walk, I could not stand, so the staff helped me to the room. It was a long wait, with head throbbing, throwing up, and wishing that I was dead and be finished with all this pain.

The clock on the wall seemed to be frozen in time and not moving. I was praying, pleading and begging God to take this pain away or take me home with him. As I had my face buried deeply into the mattress to help pressure the pain away, I suddenly heard, "Sudie, this is enough, it is time to make you better."

I looked up through a foggy cloud-like haze to see the most beautiful, handsome man or being that I had ever seen. I saw a tall frame, a beautiful smiling face, a soft soothing male voice. I replied, "Thank you."

The staff soon came in, hooked me up on an IV and started injections of needed meds. Three hours later I was feeling much better and was regaining my strength.

As I was able to talk, I began to ask the staff members about that tall good-looking doctor that had come in to see me. They appeared to be shocked at my question, and then replied that no one had come in to see me prior to them seeing me. My attending doctor would come in to check on me soon.

I knew what I had seen and what I had heard and soon everyone in the hospital emergency room had heard my story too.

Well, when my doctor did come in, he was very short and not the gorgeous man that I had seen earlier. I soon realized that yes, it was an angel, and he did not have spread out wings, but there was a heavenly aura about him.

I went home with healing and another story to write.

ANGEL ON THE BRIDGE

Many years ago, I had to learn the hard way of what was *of God* and what was *not of God*.

Stories in my other books shared some of those teachable lessons. With this statement, as a Christian, the Halloween celebration was not one that I would participate in. However, this event put a special twist on an old tradition and turned it into an alternative event for people to come tour instead of the traditional horror houses. There would be horrific scenes that would display real life situations that had resulted from making bad choices.

Back then it was called *'Hell House.'* John Neel had the brainstorm behind this idea, and it drew hundreds each night. My church was the first to literally open its doors to this new idea. I was invited to be one of the prayer warriors behind the scenes.

It was a free event offered to the public. It would continue to grow each year with more scenes created and added. John would follow the season of public interest or life situations and depict them in his scenes that always had a message to share.

People would come by buses from other towns to see this new and exciting event. The lines were always long, but when the music would start to play, you could hear only dead silence. Then the loud scary music would start. It was the signal to get ready because the new group was about to be ushered into the first scene. The tour included approximately 12 individual scenes.

There were "Spirit Guides" dressed in solid black hooded garments who looked like grim reapers. They would usher people into the needed direction toward the first scene. As each scene was over, the music would change and then the group of people would be led to the next scene. Meanwhile, loudspeakers allowed the outside waiting group to hear their screams as they would tour the inside scenes. This of course, elevated the anticipation for when it would be their time. This added to the suspense of the unknown of what they would be experiencing soon.

The first thing to experience was being pushed into a waiting stand up coffin along with several other people. It was so crammed, that you could not move. Most of the time you would find yourself almost touching face to face with a person that you have never met. Then it was dark inside that coffin and you could not see their face, but you did know one thing for sure, they were just as scared as you. Now that I have prepared you for the coming details, it is time to give some examples of what a few of the scenes visually displayed.

One of the scenes showed a bad car wreck. It would display the results of a drinking and driving situation on Prom Night. You would see bloody bodies in the demolished car, someone hanging out the windshield or laying on the ground moaning, some silent. The driver awakens to see that her friends are either dead or dying. She becomes hysterical and starts screaming. Then it is time to move to the next scene.

The next scene may be where there is an abortion taking place. It is a hospital setting with a young girl lying on the table crying. She was screaming as they appeared to be removing life-like baby parts and crudely throwing them into the bloody pan causing the red liquid to splash against the plastic screen that separates the visitors from the scene area. Suddenly she stops screaming and appears to faint or die. It is now time to move to the next scene…

In the hell scene, you see red hot walls, red-bodied beings screaming, begging and shouting warnings to make wise choices. Arms were trying to grab you or were begging for you to help them get out. They grab for you and try to warn you not to make the mistakes that they had made, but to make the right ones.

The walls looked and smelled like fire and smoke. The music sounded very evil. Just when you thought it was never going to end, a light appears above the little crosswalk bridge on the opposite side of the scene showing you the way to exit out.

After you cross the bridge, you then find yourself in the next and final scene where a bloody and beaten Jesus Christ is hanging on the Cross. As he slowly raises his head, a narrator will then ask if you want to go to Heaven or Hell. You see two doors, one labeled Heaven, and the other hell.

If you choose the heaven exit door, you will be greeted by singing angels on the other side in a bright lit up room. As you exit the door, there is an angel with a huge open book, and she asks, "Is your name in this Book of Life?" If you choose the Hell door, you will find yourself suddenly outside with no one else there, and dead silence for a few minutes... Very scary!

When this Halloween alternative first started, it was known as '*Hell House*' and then later became known as '*Final Exit*' when it began to travel around the United States.

Each year I was contacted to be part of the intercessor group. These are people who have a gift from God to see into the spiritual realm or hear and pray protection for all the actors. Sometimes an intercessor would go to the leadership staff of a group and inform them of impending trouble. During these events, members of occult groups loved to show up to make trouble, and they usually did.

I participated in this yearly outreach for several years. My gifts increased for seeing into the spiritual realm. I could see things that others could not see. This outreach was created to offer the alternative to real life situation decisions as opposed to the Halloween tradition that most were accustomed to. It was always sold out. I was in the group that stayed behind the scenes and prayed personally for some of the people that needed prayer or were even scared.

It was in the 'Hell Scene' that I saw the angel with wings standing in front of the little bridge. She was holding a big book smiling at me from a distance. I was one of the staff members that was asked to walk through scenes mingled among the visitors just in case a problem would arise. I was always very attentive to my surroundings, watching for the unexpected.

Wow, what a message. An angel in Hell? After the event was over, I found the CEO and exclaimed how real the angel looked, and that she even seemed to glow. At the end of the day, I was told that I was the only one who saw the angel. No one had been assigned to be in costume as an angel in hell.

It was during my last participation as one of the intercessors that God intervened when I was asked to lead us in prayer before the start of the event this night. As I began to pray, I could hear angelic singing and would stop praying, thinking that someone in our group was singing or that our whole prayer group was singing.

When I would pray the singing would start. When I would stop, the singing would stop. After this had taken place a couple of times, I stopped to share with the group what I was hearing. The Pastor then told me to continue. This time, I prayed while the angelic serenading continued also. After the prayer was over, they all replied that they heard it also. I was so blessed that they too were able to be blessed by this Divine Visit.

WORDS OF HEALING

My home beauty shop was doing well from the hours of 8 a.m. to 5:30 p.m. or later when needed. So, when I got a phone call telling me that there was night time job opening at one of my favorite places to visit, the Family Christian Store, I did not hesitate to inquire.

I was very familiar with this store. A friend and I went almost every Friday night to listen to the new music releases and to check out the current T-shirt sale rack. We loved these shirts because they had Bible scriptures on them.

A preacher friend of mine was close friends with the manager who had told him that she needed help. He suggested that I go put my application in. I did go and meet with the manager. She had told me to come in with my beauty shop appointment book, and I did.

She browsed through my previous and present appointments and then asked, "Why in the world would you want to come work in my store, when it appears that you are running a prosperous beauty establishment?"

I told her that it must be God's idea, because I was asking the same thing. She and I looked at my schedule and then set up my employment day to start and the hours I would work.

I loved the atmosphere. We played Christian music all day. The people that came in always had such beautiful smiling faces. They seemed to enjoy browsing in our store as much as we the employees were pleased to be there.

If I saw a person that seemed to be a little down, I would approach and offer to help if any was needed. It was that kind of freedom of speech and action store. We could talk about God, and share ministry stories without restraint.

It was on one of my night shifts that a young man came in. Even though he was smiling, you could tell that he was in pain. As I went up to him, I touched his arm and told him that the Lord had told me to pray for him because he was in pain.

A look came on his face, and the Holy Spirit whispered into my ear, 'Speak my words and they shall be healed." I then quoted the scripture from the Bible, Psalms 34:19, "Many are the afflictions of the righteous, but they shall be delivered from them all." I did not say this out loud, but the gentleman grabbed my arm and just stood there voiceless.

Once he was able to talk, he said, "Ma'am, I do not hurt anymore. I came into the store with my back hurting, and while you were talking with me, I could feel the pain leaving my body. I was being healed as you talked. I have been in pain for a long time."

I just responded with 'Praise God." I never saw that young man again.

One of the workers had heard our conversation, and I was soon being asked to pray for individual members on the staff, one by one. The stockroom closet became my prayer closet. It was during this work season at this store that I saw many movements of the Holy Spirit take place. Healing, deliverance and words of encouragement spoken. Some of those stories are recorded in my other books.

I continued to work there for about one and a half years. The store's patronage grew. Before my time was up working there, we had a Christian concert, with me organizing it. This had never been done or even considered. My heart was to showcase our local unknown music artists. Being an employee there opened many doors of opportunity to meet and feature new people of talent, ministries, authors and more.

We were limited to a certain amount of feet that the volume of the music could filter out into the busy mall without hindering the other stores. The constant flow of people still came.

People could be seen singing, dancing and talking with each other. It was like having a church concert. Curiosity seemed to be like a magnet. Some of the on-lookers soon found themselves coming in to see what was going on.

The day when I had prayed with that young man started me on a new journey of my faith walk. I soon found myself getting more comfortable about approaching people to share what the Lord would lay on my heart to say or to do.

ANGELS ON ASSIGNMENT

While on one of my Arkansas visits to see my grandmother, I was awakened to what sounded like a choir singing on this Sunday morning. I could not hear words, but I did hear beautiful music that I had never heard here on earth. There seemed to be many happy voices singing. As I sat up on my sofa where I had slept, I looked around and saw that my friend on the other sofa bed was still asleep, so I knew that this was a spiritual encounter from heaven that only I was hearing.

On this trip, odd things would happen. Like birds serenading us through open windows at night, not a normal thing. Sometimes an aroma would suddenly fill the room, noticeable to all. Sounds tapping from underneath the house, or something scratching on the roof.

I always tried to analyze these things to determine if they were real or was it just me seeing or hearing into the supernatural realm. Naturally I would share with the others when they would awaken.

My grandmother heard the singing and told us that she thought that it was us, the girls, that was singing. I was not the only one who had heard the angelic choir wake-up call.

THE GRIM REAPER

When I was working at the Family Christian Store for that short season, I would travel home in the late hours from 10 p.m. or later to go back home. I was used to seeing odd things going on at that time of night as I traveled the dark highways.

One night, I was following an 18-wheeler cab without a trailer who appeared to be trying to run the small car in front of him off the road. At first, I thought that it was friends that were playing with each other. But when I saw the big truck swerve and push the little car off toward the medium, I flashed my lights to let the big guy know that I was watching.

Inside the small compact car were two young men, high school age I would assume. They probably did something to the trucker, like show an ungodly finger motion. That I did not see, but I did see the frightened faces. The little car sped up and so did the trucker and me in close pursuit. There were no cell phones at that time.

I was hoping it would end, but then the little car drove fast through a McDonald's drive-thru, and the trucker did also, very dangerously. They both came out, and that is when I flashed my bright lights several times again to warn the trucker to leave them alone. He did and sped on as I was trying to write down his license number in case this would end up in an accident.

Nothing was on the news the next day about any accident, so I guess that everything turned out alright and the kids learned a lesson if one needed to be learned.

However, the next afternoon, as I was headed to work for 6 p.m., I saw a figure walking on the overpass going in the same direction as myself, but he was not your normal pedestrian. He wore a long black flowing cloak with a hood over its head. He seemed over-dressed since this was in the heat of the summer. He was walking very slow while looking down, then to his left, then to his right. I had slowed down to see his face, but there was none to be seen. I then realized that he looked like the Grim Reaper that we are accustomed to seeing in films or picture books.

I went on to work. I got off around 10 p.m. that night and had to cross that overpass. He was not around, but I felt strange as I drove across it. There have been many wrecks on that overpass, and I have had a few close calls myself.

I am always braking to let the person behind me know to slow down, when the traffic light at the bottom of the hill has turned red. I have almost been hit in the back several times. If I did not have to take that route, I would not. As I am sitting in my car, I can see signs of many colors of paint on the cement sides of this overpass. I wondered if that is why I saw what I saw. I never saw him again and glad of it.

TRAILING SPIRITS

Many years ago, a friend and I had visited this church. The Pastor was well experienced in exposing the different occult practices in our area. Satanic groups were infiltrating churches, even mine with people sharing false and dangerous doctrines.

This was during the time that I was learning more about the different gifts that I was experiencing from the Holy Spirit. Not all churches believe in this doctrine, so I needed to find outlets for clarification of why I could see evil forms among us, or smell different aromas that would suddenly enter the room, as well as extreme temperature changes in a room, suddenly getting very cold. In many of my previous stories, I did share what I would come to learn through different journeys.

Fast forward to 2016. I now find myself blessed with a Christian friend who is also a publisher of many books. We were friends connected by our faith. As we grew closer, he would ask questions that I had already written a story about but were not yet published. He began to question me on some of my stories because he was desiring a closer walk of faith into the supernatural realm of the Godly kind.

It was I who suggested that we go to a service at this church. I was not even sure if the Pastor would remember me. I was a little nervous but tried to hide it from my friend. I anticipated that something was going to take place in the supernatural realm. Of course, he was hoping that it would.

I always sat in the back rows when visiting a new church in case something would happen. Prior to the service starting, a word of encouragement was shared with the congregation and people were praying. The Pastor came from the front to where we sat and I reintroduced myself from many years ago. He also prayed for me to be successful in sharing my books.

It was during the praise and worship that I suddenly heard a crackling sound. I turned to see how close we were to the sound system thinking perhaps it was coming from their system.

I then felt a fluttering of something over my head. I turned to see a large tall man in a white shirt standing directly behind me. Maybe it was his shirt that the air condition system was blowing it on me. Then I looked back and he was no longer there. I then leaned forward and placed myself on the edge of my seat and folded my hands and began to pray once more.

Again, suddenly I heard a loud grunting in my left ear. I had heard this sound before, and it was definitely evil. I turned to see but saw no one. At the end of the service, my friend did ask me what had happened. I later told him on the way home.

Now I knew that this church lined up with God, and felt that somehow an evil spirit had entered on someone to get in. Later I discovered that it was me. Earlier that day I interviewed an author on my TV program. Her books touched on the areas of rituals in the Egyptian days. She was into fantasy and had come to talk about her book. I was hoping that she would not show up for the interview, but she did.

I had that book on the book shelf at my house. For those of you that do not understand, bad things can come upon us if we allow an opening for it to enter, especially from the demonic realm. This is called "trailing spirits." I did not get rid of the book, and I did not read it. I had thought about giving it away, but that was not the right thing to do. I either had to burn it or just pray against what it stood for. I did not burn it.

The scripture speaks of burning occult items here: "Many of them also which used curious arts brought their books together and burned them before all men: and they counted the price of them and found it fifty thousand pieces of silver." Acts 19:19

The gift of hearing into the spiritual world is what this story is about. There is nothing I can do but pray and seek the Lord for revelation or guidance. He always brings me understanding.

THE IMP

Sometimes I get invitations to go and become a part of a newly formed organization. My friend and I would go and film and then share on Youtube for more exposure.

The guest speakers would sometimes want us to participate in little exercises that were becoming more and more uncomfortable for me. The church doctrine that we both follow does not believe in psychic practices of any kind. I was beginning to sense that my friend and I should not continue to come and film these sessions. We had attended maybe three before the following happened.

The organizer seemed to be aware of our discomfort as we huddled in the back with the camera rolling. One of the members had approached me with an invitation to come and have a psychic session with him. I tried to politely reject him and turn the conversation away from the topic. He became pushy, so I just thanked him for the invite and declined the invite.

At the end of the meeting, I informed my friend that we needed to talk when the camera audio was off. The man again came to me, but this time his face was very red and he seemed to be very angry at me. As he spoke to me, his face began to become contorted and his ears got pointed and he has big bulging eyes with a wide evil grin.

He was trying to plead his case that there was nothing wrong with what he did for a living. This time I told him while looking directly into his huge eyes that I did not believe in what he was doing and therefore I would not participate and once more declined. My friend and I then got up and left the room as fast as we could.

I asked my friend if he had noticed that the features had changed on the man? He said no. A name come into my thoughts, the word "imp." I recalled seeing a picture in my Bible and he looked just like it. When I got home, I took my Bible out and yes, there it was. My friend and I decided to separate ourselves from any future meetings or obligations to film for this group. The organizer got very angry and responded to us by very hateful emails. The angrier that she got, the clearer it became that we were not to be involved.

Prior to going to the first meeting, the Holy Spirit had prompted me to give her a set of my four books, 'The Spiritual Warfare Series.' If she had read the books, then she would have understood why we both chose to stop coming to her meetings. I was able to remind her once again that I had given them to her to read so that she would know more about my faith walk.

In the end, we may have been in the new group of a witch's den. When the imp showed up, that was our cue to never attend again. We had to block her ugly messages. She finally left us alone.

CRACKING BONES

A young Christian woman needed serious prayer. My prayer partner, Neal, called to see if I could come meet them at a nearby location to pray with them. He had been ministering by phone to her for a while and decided that he would like for me to join them.

My home was nearby, so I suggested that they come to my house so that it would be more private for all. I knew this lady and if she was asking for prayer, then I wanted to help in any way that I could.

The lady and I had been wanting to get together for coffee for some time, but our schedules never lined up. They were soon at my place and I invited them in.

As they entered, I could sense a heaviness in the air. Within the last year I had noticed a change in her demeanor. She always looked so tired, but she would manage to smile anyway. I knew in my spirit that something had changed in her life, and whatever it was, was physically draining her. My prayer partner had been ministering to her for several months as she shared her heart on different topics.

The first words out of her mouth were, "I guess he told you what has been going on in my life."

I replied, "No, not at all, other than to lift you up in prayer."

As she sat down in the cushioned chair, and my friend sat on the sofa near her, I chose to sit in a chair across from them. I was being quieter than usual while asking for revelation and guidance from the Holy Spirit as I listened to some shocking details coming from her.

The time came to pray. I got up to stand behind the chair that I had been sitting in. I was going to let him continue to take the lead in prayer, but he asked me to come join hands and pray.

Before I joined holding hands to pray, I notice that her hands were beginning to stretch out in a very unusual way. As I noticed her hands changing, she began to explain that when the Holy Spirit would come upon her, that her hands would stretch out with the knuckles turning white and she could not even pick up her purse. Others would have to assist her and escort her to her car. She would sometimes have to drive home in this condition. I knew that this was not of God.

My friend started speaking in tongues, which is an unknown heavenly prayer language. This is a prayer language that Satan cannot understand. I could see that once he was finished that she had the questioning look on her face of not understanding its purpose. I then went and pulled out my Bible to find the scripture that shared the gifts of the Holy Spirit and wrote them down for her.

Some get this gift right automatically, while others may receive it later. As I held both of her hands cradled in mine while he prayed, I could feel a resistance of her trying to pull them from me. I just held on firm, but gentle and could feel the cracking of bones as her hands softened up and became warm.

I could hear in the spiritual realm that this curse was leaving. I remember us quoting the Bible verse that says, "They shall lay hands on the sick and they shall recover." If she could not use her hands, then this was not from God. It was now time for her to head back home.

Several weeks later, I did ask her if her hands were still doing that stiffening thing, and she said that it never happened again after we had prayed for her. Hallelujah!

THE SEER GIFT

There is a ministry that has meetings in a hotel in a nearby town. My friend is active in this ministry. He invited me a few times to go with him. I was not looking for a new church, but I finally accepted and went out of respect to him.

I did not feel uncomfortable and everything spoken seemed to line up with God's Word. It was titled a Seer Workshop, a meeting for those who have the gift of being a seer, and my friend believes that I am a seer. A seer is a person who can see into the spiritual realm, which I do. It is in the Bible.

I soon found out that my gift does not work in the exact same way as those that were present that day. Some were able to just touch you and suddenly they were speaking and praying what they were seeing.

When my gift gets ready to operate, I will sense that something is soon going to take place. I will then get very quiet. I ask for spiritual eyes to see. I always ask the Lord to guide me if there should be anything that He wants me to see or say to guide me. I cannot just lay hands and BAM!... a screen of action appears and directs me what to do. My gift does not work exactly like that.

After being there all day, I was tired and ready to go home. I had tried to not bring any attention to myself and just be an observer. Great prophetic words were spoken to me by different people.

Just when I thought my supernatural seer gift was not going to manifest, I then noticed something forming on the pastor's face. I looked at his face as he sat in his chair. I asked, "Lord, what am I supposed to be seeing?" I then clearly saw a mask forming on his face. I looked once more to see that it had now gotten darker. He looked like he had just tied a mask to his face that resembled that of a raccoon.

I asked my friend if he saw anything on the face of the Pastor, and he said no. I then asked God what was wrong? The Holy Spirit responded and said that he was sick and needed prayer for healing. I asked for permission to place my hands around his eyes and then I cuddled his face in my hands. It was not necessary for me to pray out loud.

I did share this with the Pastor as my friend stood near me. I was following the directions from the Holy Spirit as they were being given to me. The Pastor seemed to receive a needed touch of healing as this was done. I do not remember what he said, but I do recall that he confirmed that he had been ill but had come to preach anyway.

God showed up and my gift of healing was activated.

CONCLUSION

(The following sections were written by Neal Bertrand, the editor and publisher of this book.)

You may have a dream or the desire to operate in the same gifts of the Holy Spirit that we operate in, but God gives the gifts according to His will. We recommend that you seek God with all of your heart for His perfect will for your life. As you seek God's will, He will reveal the gifts that He has already given you and what gifts He wants to give you.

We cannot force God's hand. We cannot force God to give us the gifts that we want. All we can do is pray, seek God with all of our heart and be obedient to His Word and allow God to direct our paths.

WHAT DOES GOD LOOK LIKE?

One day as I was lying on my bed praying, I told the Lord that I wanted to see Him, I wanted to see what He really looked like. I immediately got a response inside of me which was, "I'm in the Book. You can see what I look like there."

So I started looking through my Bible and I was astonished to see such descriptive language about how God looked when He appeared to people. Following are some examples.

In the book of the prophet Ezekiel, the prophet is entertaining guests in his home in Babylon, when God appears before him and transports him to Jerusalem.

Ezekiel 8.2 Then I beheld, and lo a likeness as the appearance of fire: from the appearance of his loins even downward, fire; and from his loins even upward, as the appearance of brightness, as the colour of amber.

The color of amber is a golden yellow color, the same color as liquid, molten metal being poured into a pot.

In chapter one of Ezekiel, he sees the throne of God coming down from Heaven, with fire enfolding the throne, with lightning and thunder, and a tornado of fire. A very impressive and awesome sight! The throne was blue with a man sitting upon it. The man on the throne was the same that appeared in his home ... legs of fire and a torso of amber. Who is this entity? This is Jesus before he took on a flesh and blood body and was born of a virgin.

Moses was tending the sheep when God appeared to him as a large flame of fire in a burning bush.

Later, on Mount Sinai, God came down in a flame of fire, with the mountain smoking like a furnace, with ear-piercing trumpet blasts, thunder and lightning flashes, with the mountain experiencing an earthquake. God met with Moses and the elders of Israel and they had supper with Jehovah God Almighty there on the mountaintop. Yes, this too, is a description of Jesus before he took on a flesh and blood body and was born of a virgin. Jesus is the Almighty God! Jesus is Jehovah, or Yahweh, however you want to spell it.

Later, God was manifest in the flesh and walked among mankind. It is recorded in the Bible that when Jesus went to the top of a mountain with the apostles Peter, James and John, that His Divine Nature was revealed.

Mat 17:2 And was transfigured before them: and his face did shine as the sun, and his raiment was white as the light.

This is Jesus Christ, the same being that appeared to Ezekiel and Moses, that the prophet Daniel saw (in Daniel chapter 7), and that walked with Adam and Eve in the Garden of Eden.

Jesus was, and still is the manifestation of Love and Grace. He volunteered to come down to this place called Earth, become an offering for our sins, and take away our sin and disease. Jesus is God's free love gift to us. Believe it. FEAR NOT! Receive Him into your heart so you can be granted eternal salvation and be rescued from an eternity in hell.

WHERE WILL YOU LIVE AFTER YOU DIE?

You will live forever. Did you know that?

No, not your physical body that you live in. Your body is not the real you. The real "you" is your spirit and soul, your personality, thoughts, feelings and emotions ... which lives in your human body. Your human spirit and soul will live forever somewhere ... but where?

So the question remains, where will you live after you die?

Some think that because their parents were a certain religion, or devoutly followed a religious tradition, that will guarantee them a place in Heaven. Not true.

No amount of prayer to the saints or Blessed Virgin can get you into Heaven.

What makes you think that the Heavenly Father God will allow you into Heaven?

Neither will going to a church, or doing good deeds, or being good enough or buying your way in. Nope! No amount of money or being good enough can get you into Heaven. If all that were true, then Jesus Christ came down from Heaven and died on the cross in vain... all for nothing.

If you want to join a club or organization, you must sign-up, or enroll, and pay the membership fee. Only then will you be granted access. Gate crashers are not allowed in.

If you want to live in Heaven after you die, you must enroll first, and the membership fee must be paid. The membership fee is extremely expensive. That fee to get in is the blood of God's son, Jesus Christ. By his shed blood He provided a bundle of benefits. Jesus offered Himself on the cross as a living sacrifice to pay for your salvation, your healing, and your righteousness with God.

Your name must be written in Heaven before you die. But the catch is that your membership fee has already been paid on your behalf as a free love gift to you. What you need to do is believe it and receive it. If you do not believe and receive it, you are rejecting God's Son. The only place for those folks is to live in hell with the devil and his evil demons. That is NOT God's plan for you.

DO YOU WANT TO LIVE FOREVER WITH GOD?

Jesus has made a way for you to be set free from the devil. Jesus said the devil is a liar, a deceiver, and a murderer.

If you have read this book and are not sure whether you have a place reserved in heaven for you and have been born again, as Jesus said in John chapter 3, please consider doing so now.

If you receive Jesus, you have everything to gain and nothing to lose. But if you reject Him, you have nothing to gain and everything to lose.

My friend, Jesus loves you and cares for you. Had it not been for the grace of God, the devil would have killed you long ago. God is giving you a chance to get saved. Jesus loves you. That's why He came to earth and died on the cross to wash away your sins with His precious Blood! Jesus Christ the Messiah wants to set you free by coming into your heart.

If you pray this prayer with an honest, sincere heart, Jesus will hear you and will definitely save you from Hell and make you a child of God and take you to heaven when you die.

PRAY THIS PRAYER TO GO TO HEAVEN

"Lord Jesus, I ask you to forgive me of all my sins, and come into my heart, and make me a new person. I am willing to repent and turn from my sins. I receive you Jesus, as my Savior, and I confess with my mouth that Jesus is my Lord, and Messiah, to the Glory of God the Father. Amen."

YOUR ASSURANCE OF SALVATION

John 3:3 Jesus answered and said unto him, Verily, verily I say unto thee, Except a man be born again, he cannot see the kingdom of God.

4 Nicodemus saith unto him. How can a man be born when he is old? Can he enter the second time into his mother's womb, and be born?

5 Jesus answered, Verily, verily, I say unto thee, Except a man be born of water and of the spirit, he cannot enter into the kingdom of God.

6 That which is born of the flesh is flesh; and that which is born of the Spirit is spirit.

7 Marvel not that I said unto thee, Ye must be born again.

John 3:16 For God so loved the world that he gave his only begotten Son, that whosoever believeth in him should not perish, but have everlasting life.

17 For God sent not his Son into the world to condemn the world: but that the world through him might be saved.

18 He that believeth on him is not condemned: but he that believeth not is condemned already, because he hath not believed in the name of the only begotten Son of God.

19 And this is the condemnation, that light is come into the world, and men loved darkness rather than light, because their deeds were evil.

20 For every one that doeth evil hateth the light, neither cometh to the light, lest his deeds should be reproved.

21 But he that doeth truth cometh to the light, that his deeds may be manifest, that they are wrought in God.

John 1:10 He (Jesus) was in the world, and the world was made by him, and the world knew him not.

11 He came unto his own, and his own received him not.

12 But as many as received him, to them gave he power to become the sons of God, even to them that believe on his name.

Colossians 1:12 Giving thanks unto the Father, which hath made us able to be partakers of the inheritance of the saints in light:

13 Who hath delivered us from the power of darkness, and hath translated us into the kingdom of his dear Son:

14 In whom we have redemption through his blood, even the forgiveness of sins.

Luke 13:3 I tell you, Nay: But, except ye repent, ye shall all likewise perish.

John 8:24 I said therefore unto you, that ye shall die in your sins: for if you believe not that I am He, ye shall die in your sins.

Ephesians 2:8 For by grace are ye saved through faith: and that not of yourselves: it is the gift of God.

9 Not of works, lest any man should boast.

Romans 10: 9 That if thou shalt confess with thy mouth the Lord Jesus, and shalt believe in thine heart that God hath raised him from the dead, thou shall be saved.

10 For with the heart man believeth unto righteousness; and with the mouth confession is made unto salvation.

13 For whosoever shall call upon the name of the Lord shall be saved.

John 14:6 Jesus saith unto him, I am the way, the truth, and the life: no man cometh unto the Father, but by me.

Philippians 2:9 Wherefore God also hath highly exalted him, and given him a name which is above every name:

10 That at the name of Jesus every knee should bow, of things in heaven, and things in earth, and things under the earth;

11 And that every tongue should confess that Jesus Christ is Lord, to the glory of God the Father.

Acts 4:12 Neither is there salvation in any other: for there is none other name under heaven given among men, whereby we must be saved.

ABOUT THE AUTHOR

Sudie Landry was born in February 1949 in Natchez, Mississippi to a truck-driving father and a stay-at-home mom with six small children. Life for her and her siblings suddenly changed, and they were placed into a state foster home for three years.

This is where her faith began to grow as a small child, as she learned to pray and believe the preaching that she heard at church. Little did she know that this would start her unique life journey into the supernatural realm.

It was during this three-year period in the late 1950s that she began to see things that no one else seemed to be aware of. She knew some things ahead of time before they happened. She could sense impending danger, and smell odors that she could not describe. She did not tell anyone, but just said a simple prayer to not be afraid and that the bad things would not happen.

She has been in many valleys of abuse. She knows what it is like to have three near-death experiences, to lose a child by the error of another, to be verbally and physically abused, raped as a small child, and stay in an abusive marriage of 45 years. Her faith in God and the power of prayer prepared her to face supernatural encounters of the heavenly, Godly kind, and the demonic manifestations recorded in her stories. Her favorite scripture is "And Jesus looking upon them saith, With men it is impossible, but not with God: for with God all things are possible." (Mark 10:27)

For many years she produced the TV show "Louisiana Heartbeats," which can be viewed on her YouTube channel "Louisiana Heart Beats You Tube Channel." She is also the president of the Writers' Guild of Acadiana, encouraging writers to attain their full potential.

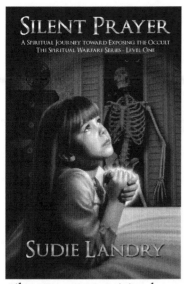

Silent Prayer: A Spiritual Journey Toward Exposing the Occult – $14.95

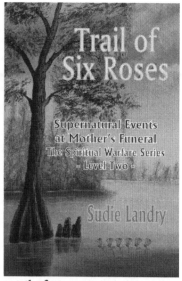

Trail of Six Roses: Supernatural Events at Mother's Funeral – $6.95

Mom Bradley's Crossover: From Deathbed to Heaven – $8.95

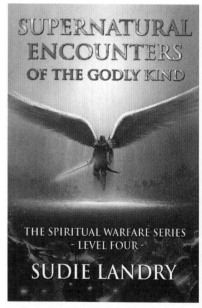

Supernatural Encounters of the Godly Kind – $14.95

 Down-Home Cajun Cooking Favorites

 Slow Cooker Meals: Easy Home Cooking for Busy People

 Dad's War Photos: Adventures in the South Pacific

 Rice Cooker Meals: Fast Home Cooking for Busy People

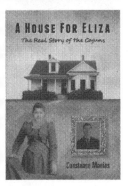 A House For Eliza: The Real Story of the Cajuns

 Never Say Goodbye: Real Stories of the Cajuns

 From Cradle to Grave: Journey of the Louisiana Orphan Train Riders

 Cajun Country Fun Coloring & Activity Book (Bilingual English/ French)

Louisiana Legacy: History of the Daigle and Schexnayder Families

The Real You, My Beloved: Seeing Yourself Through God's Eyes

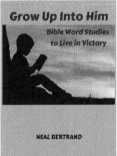

Grow Up Into Him: Bible Word Studies to Live in Victory

Fun Times Puzzle & Activity Book

Fun Times Cajun Puzzle & Activity Book

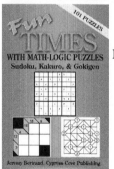

Fun Times with Math-Logic Puzzles Sudoku, Kakuro, & Gokigen

All the Scriptures You Need to Know ABOUT THE LAST DAYS

Made in the USA
Middletown, DE
10 August 2020